COSPLAY
Crash Course

COSPLAY
Crash Course

**A complete guide to designing cosplay
wigs, makeup and accessories**

Mina "Mistiqarts" Petrović

IMPACT

CONTENTS

1 Getting Started 10

Ready to jump into the exciting world of cosplay? This chapter will help you choose your character, look for references and get started building your costume.

2 Sewing and Crafting 16

Learn to navigate the vast world of cosplay costume materials including fabric, thermoplastics and the basics of sewing. Then follow the lessons to make some awesome, easy props of your own.

3 Makeup and Wigs 66

This section focuses on your head and skin—specifically your face (makeup) and hair (wigs and styling). Also covered are cool tips on fake tattoos, fake blood and body painting.

4 Promoting Your Cosplay 96

Once you have your character's costume, personality and looks nailed down, it's time to self-promote. This chapter covers every-thing you need to know about photography, from shooting pictures to posing for them, as well as cosplay convention etiquette.

WHAT YOU NEED

acrylic paint
alcohol wipes
assorted fabrics
black permanent marker
black spray paint
body paint
cardboard
card stock
contact cement
craft foam
craft wire
duct tape
elastic bands
EVA foam
fabric adhesive
gel pens
glue gun
glue sticks
heat gun
makeup
makeup brushes and sponges
needle and thread
paint brushes
paper tape
scissors

My name is Mimi! I will be your helpful guide through this book.

Introduction

Has a fictional character ever influenced you so much that you had the unstoppable urge to be that character for a day? Do you love costumes and crafting but don't know where to begin? There was a time when it was considered strange to dabble in cosplay, but today it is considered a fun and enjoyable activity. It's a hobby you can share with your loved ones, and a way to meet new friends and learn artistic and crafting skills. In cosplay, you can do things you never thought possible and boost your confidence by finding like-minded people to share your experiences with. And that is exactly what this book is all about.

I have met amazing and talented friends during my life in cosplay. Together, we want to show you how to learn from our triumphs as well as our mistakes, and to share our little hacks and shortcuts to make detailed costumes you can be proud of. We gladly pass this knowledge along to you because the cosplay community is all about sharing and helping each other. We hope you'll find this guide helpful and uplifting, and that you will use it as inspiration for creating many of your own cosplay costumes and creative projects.

Lets begin our journey!

MEET THE CREW!

This book was created in cooperation with nine international cosplay artists who share the common goal of introducing you to the world of cosplay while promoting inclusivity and body positivity. This diverse group of individuals will share their stories and help you kick off your new hobby with all the helpful advice they can offer.

Artist: ByALady Costumes
Name: Brandy Cross
Location: Netherlands
Instagram: @byaladycostumes
Bio: Brandy Cross is a writer and costume designer with a passion for alternative history comics, fabric and costume-making. She fell in love with the designing, creating and sewing aspects of cosplay—bringing an idea or a character to life with dozens of tiny details. For Brandy, cosplay is about creativity, learning, friendship and fun, which is why she often works with groups to design and create costumes for everyone.

Artist: EDGE CAP Cosplay
Name: Kenichi Nakayama
Location: Japan
Instagram: @ken__edgecap
Bio: Kenichi Nakayama is a cosplayer based in Japan. He began cosplaying in 2014. His biggest motivation is to prove himself by producing the highest-quality cosplay costumes—as close to the level of movie costumes as possible.

Artist: Ferasha Cosplay
Name: Isidora Vlasak
Location: Serbia
Instagram: @ferashacosplay

Bio: Isidora Vlasak is known on the Internet by her pseudonym, Ferasha (Arabic for *butterfly*). She speaks several languages and works as an interpreter for various international organizations. Her true passion, however, is the geek culture. She's a panelist, blogger, reviewer, podcaster, event organizer, workshop facilitator, fan fiction writer, and cosplayer. She loves to travel, loathes boring clothes, prefers dogs to cats, obsesses over *Game of Thrones*, always roots for the Dark Side and dislikes happy endings. (Except in real life.) She has been cosplaying since 2010, emphasizing visual transformation and acting in character. She loves cosplaying villains best because she thinks they have cooler personalities and a better fashion sense. Ferasha lives in Belgrade, Serbia, with her husband and their dog. She also happens to be in her late 30s—as the saying goes, you're never too old to do what you love.

Artist: Rado Raven Art
Name: Radoslav Petrov
Location: Bulgaria
Instagram: @radoravenart

Bio: Radoslav Petrov's friends call him Rado for short. He is a dental technician by trade and an artist by heart. Painting, crafting, designing, sewing and acting are the ways he brings more color to his everyday life. He has never taken acting lessons, but he developed his theatrical skills by watching his favorite actors and then imitating them in front of a mirror. He is inspired by nature and loves to read. Some of his favorite fantasy novels include *The Lord of the Rings*; *A Song of Ice and Fire* and *Harry Potter*. The magic and freedom to be whomever or whatever he wants is what drew him to cosplay. Rado's best advice for beginning cosplayers is to take risks, don't be afraid to experiment and let your imagination go wild.

Artist: Marijana Miletić, Cosplay Crafter
Name: Marijana Miletić
Location: Serbia
Instagram: @marijana.miletic
Bio: Marijana Miletić is a sculptor by trade, a jeweler and a convention photographer. While not a cosplayer herself, she enjoys crafting costumes and props for others. She loves to see people take a sword or wand in their hands and be instantly transformed into their favorite character.

Artist: Rebel Among The Stars
Name: Laura Ducros
Location: United States
Instagram: @rebelats
Bio: Laura Ducros is a cosplayer, crafter, organizer, competitor, contest judge and spreader of cospositivity (cosplay positivity). Her passion for cosplay was ignited in 2007 when she attended her first convention. It began with a store-bought anime costume and turned into an obsession with fully crafted armor. Being a part of multiple cosplay groups has helped shape the costumes she creates today. Laura enjoys keeping the cosplay community growing by sharing her knowledge with future cosplayers.

Artist: Tenshi Cosplay
Name: Jovana Ninković
Location: Serbia
Instagram: @tenshi_senpie
Bio: Jovana Ninković has loved costuming and playing dress up for as long as she can remember, but it wasn't until 2013 that she first attempted to reproduce a specific design. Over time, she started making costumes more regularly. The more complex her designs became, the more fun she had making costumes. She enjoys every part of the process and is proud to be involved in every single aspect of her cosplay, from planning to photo editing. Jovana says the best thing cosplay has given her is the team of friends she gets to have fun with.

Artist: Twinfools Cosplay
Name: Lucas Wilson
Location: Canada
Instagram: @twinfools
Bio: Lucas Wilson is known online and in the cosplay community by his cosplay name, Twinfools. He's had the honor of seeing the cosplay community change and grow over the ten years he has been cosplaying. He has traveled the world and met people of all identities, cultures and abilities who share his love of cosplay. His primary goal through cosplay is to increase and open up accessibility of the hobby to make it something that anyone can partake in. He's experienced the transformative and confidence-boosting power of cosplay firsthand, and he wants to ensure that everyone has that same access and opportunity. Outside of cosplay, Lucas' other passions include LGBTQ+ rights advocacy, sports/fitness and video games.

Artist: Mistiqarts Cosplay
Name: Mina Petrović
Location: Serbia
Instagram: @mistiqartscosplay
Bio: Mina Petrović has been a convention organizer, book author and cosplay judge, as well a body positivity activist and teacher for the past ten years. What inspires her most is the smiling people she sees at conventions, as they get out of their comfort zones and make new friends. Working with young people and starry-eyed, driven individuals who fight for cospositivity is her passion.

What is Cosplay?

Cosplay is a popular hobby that involves dressing up as characters from movies, TV shows, books, comics, video games, anime, manga and even original stories. Many people who cosplay also enjoy acting out scenes involving the characters. The cosplay community strives to be one of acceptance—a safe space for people of all ages, genders, races and body types.

There are many ways to put together a cosplay costume. You can buy a pre-made costume, combine regular clothes into a costume, or craft and build a costume from scratch. However you choose to cosplay, the most important thing to remember is to have fun!

Cosplay is a combination of the words costume and play!

The Rules of Cosplay

1. Always ask for permission to take photos of a cosplayer.
2. Cosplay is for everyone.
3. Pick a costume you like, a character you enjoy and HAVE FUN!

Choosing a Character

Picking out the perfect character is the fun first step of cosplay. In a sea of characters, we often choose the ones whose stories impress us the most. So what should you consider when making your decision? Here are a few helpful tips and ideas to keep in mind when you're deciding who to be.

What Are Your Motivations?
- Popularity or trendiness of a character
- Character's particular look (beautiful, scary, etc.)
- Desire to be a part of a cosplay group of friends
- Challenge of the character design
- Character looks like you physically

Put Your Own Spin On It
Cosplay is more than just a lookalike hobby; you are free to be creative with your own versions of existing characters, and even cosplay your own unique characters. In cosplay there are no boundaries regarding gender, color palettes or mixing topics together.

In addition, knowing and becoming your beloved character is another special essence of cosplay. Role playing with other fans of the character can be one of the most fun parts.

Plan Your Budget

Cosplay can be a pricey hobby, so plan your budget wisely. While it is possible to make costumes out of affordable or recycled materials, some details like shoes, wigs and makeup can be quite expensive. So when you are selecting a character, try to take your own looks into consideration. For example, if your hair is a similar length or color to your character, you may not need to purchase a wig. I recommend making a budget to see where you can afford to spend a little extra, then get creative and thrifty with different aspects of your designs.

Gathering References

References are important when researching a costume. Your references will show you every precise shape and detail of a character's appearance. Some great places to gather references are art books, footage and screen shots from film or television shows, official concept art, fan websites, official action figures, fan art from sites like DeviantArt and photos of other cosplayers who have dressed as the character.

Plan Ahead

The Internet is wonderful resource for finding costumes and materials to build them. If you are going to order some or all of your costume online, make sure to plan ahead so everything you need arrives before your next event.

Cosplay Tips and Tricks

The character you choose to cosplay may be outfitted with big and bold shapes or large costuming details. Be mindful when planning a costume with non-human features like big wings, extra limbs, horns, etc. Make sure these aspects of your costume are not too sharp or heavy so that you won't injure yourself or others.

You should also plan to create costumes with soft and lightweight materials. You want your outfit to be comfortable to wear for many hours. Before wearing the costume at a convention or event, stress-test everything to make sure any important parts will not fall off in a crowd.

Here are a few other tips and tricks you find useful when putting together your cosplay character…

Lengthy Costumes Can Be Limiting
Plan accordingly for the event you're attending. Long capes, dresses and wigs don't go well with stairs and crowded areas.

Hey guys, wait for me!

Mobility Is Important
Plan to be able to move in your costume, especially if you will be on your feet for a while during a gathering.

Don't Forget the Pockets!
It can be useful if your costume has built-in pockets or bags.

Makeup Is Appropriate for Everyone

Fictional characters often have unique or colorful facial and body features that you must use makeup to re-create. Since cosplay is a form of performance art, makeup is completely appropriate for anyone who wishes to use it.

Consider the Season and Weather

Make sure to plan for summer or winter weather conditions before deciding on a costume design.

Fashion Tape and Sock Glue

Double-sided fashion tape is a must-have to help clothes stick tightly to the skin. Roll-on body adhesive (also known as sock glue) is also helpful to keep knee socks in place. You can find both online or at your local drugstore.

Make Sure You Can Move!

Fictional characters often have unrealistic costumes that would not move well in real life. It is up to you to make changes that will help you move freely and allow the costume to fit as comfortably as possible.

Undergarments in Cosplay

To get started, let's go over some options for what to wear under the costume itself. Undergarments can provide comfort as well as a more effective transformation. However, adding layers under your costume can also make you feel too warm, so plan accordingly and stay hydrated.

Pantyhose/Sheer Tights

For smooth and shiny legs, pantyhose make all the difference. If your character has socks, especially thigh-high or over-the-knee, I recommend sewing them onto the pantyhose fabric to keep them from rolling down.

Dance Belt

A dance belt is a specialized undergarment commonly worn by male ballet dancers to support the groin area. When wearing a skintight costume, this is something to consider for personal comfort.

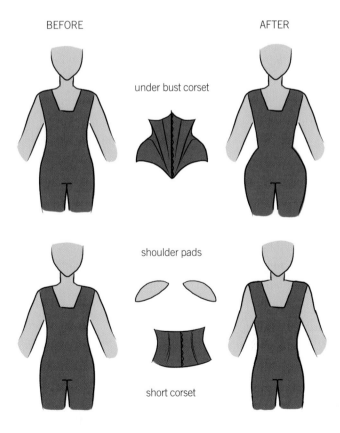

BEFORE

AFTER

under bust corset

shoulder pads

short corset

Body Shapers

Body shapers under your costume are an option and can drastically transform your look. Try combining shapers with corsets or shoulder pads for new looks and shapes. However, you should not feel it is mandatory to alter your body shape for cosplay. Your body is beautiful as it is and you should dress however you feel most comfortable and confident! If you have respiratory or other health issues, please prioritize your health and avoid obstructive costumes.

Fabric Basics

Fabric is one of the most important aspects of a cosplay costume. The main divide among fabrics is between natural and synthetic. Natural fabrics are more expensive, but they help your skin breathe and feel comfortable. Synthetic fabrics often look and feel natural, but they can cause you to overheat. Here are a few fabric options commonly used in cosplay.

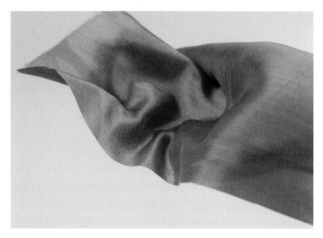

Lining Fabric

Lining fabric is inexpensive and ideal for inside a costume or for filling in large areas like the underside of a ball gown. Lining fabric is not recommended as a main material because it's too shiny and prone to ripping.

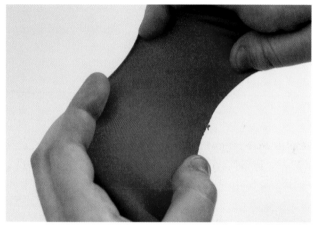

Elastane

Elastane fabric is often used for skintight costumes due to its flexibility, but it can be tricky to sew on account of its thinness. Lycra and Spandex are both common brands of elastane.

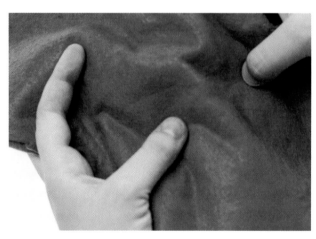

Wool Felt

Wool felt can be precisely and easily cut, glued and sewn. It is an easy fabric to work with, but it is thick and not breathable.

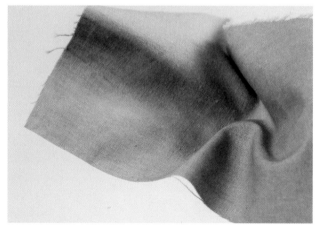

Cotton Fabric

Regular cotton fabric is just rigid enough for tailored costumes with a sharp design. It can sometimes contain elastane to give it some stretch.

Quick Fixes for Frayed Synthetic Fabric

Problem: Frayed Edge
Synthetic fabric can sometimes fray or fall apart where you cut it.

Quick Fix 1: Nail Polish
Apply transparent nail polish to seal the edges.

Quick Fix 2: Seared Edge
Burn the edges with a match to sear them into a smooth edge.

Specialty Fabrics

Tulle (fine net or mesh fabric common in wedding gowns and veils), organdy (a lightweight, sheer, stiff fabric used on the inside of garments to stiffen them, such as collars and cuffs), faux leather and pillow stuffing are all useful fabrics to achieve unique visual effects for cosplay. You can find these fabrics online, at craft or fabric stores, and even at furniture or upholstery stores. Remember, if your skin reacts badly to certain fabrics, avoid using them in costumes.

Types of Glue

There are many different types of glue that can be used on a variety of materials. Always make sure to work in a ventilated area or with a mask on for safety. Here are some common glues used for affixing costumes and props.

Glue Gun
The most universally used tool in cosplay is probably the hot glue gun. Melted plastic can be affixed to many materials. It can also be used to sculpt shapes and pieces of a costume.

Super Glue
Super glue is a must-have for emergency fixes at a convention. It can even help in styling wigs. Just remember not to touch it directly.

Contact Cement
Contact cement is a multipurpose neoprene rubber adhesive great for connecting non-porous surfaces. It's strong and permanent, but you must let it set first.

Wallpaper Paste
Wallpaper paste can be used to create a lightweight glue mixture perfect for papier-mâché props.

Wood Glue
Wood glue can be used for patching surfaces, styling wigs and creating smooth surfaces on your props and costumes.

Sock Glue

Sock glue is a roll-on body adhesive that's great for getting socks to stick to your clothes and skin. It's also washable.

Spirit Gum

Spirit gum is an adhesive used to stick on wigs, moustaches and other fake body hair.

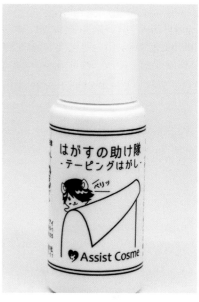

Glue Remover

For strong glue like spirt gum, it's important to have a glue remover or solvent on hand that is gentle on the skin.

Double-Sided Tape

Double-sided tape can help hold your wig or mask (and even your clothing) in place.

Face Lift Tape

Face lift tape is used to lift or modify the face before putting on a wig.

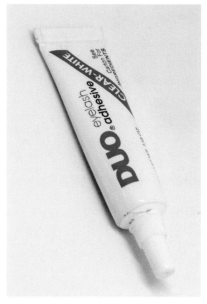

Lash Glue

Lash adhesive is great for affixing eyelashes, gluing down wig sideburns, wigs and other details to the skin.

Thermoplastics

Thermoplastic is a type of plastic that becomes soft when heated and hard when cooled down. Thermoplastic materials are great for shaping and sculpting costume elements such as armor and other props.

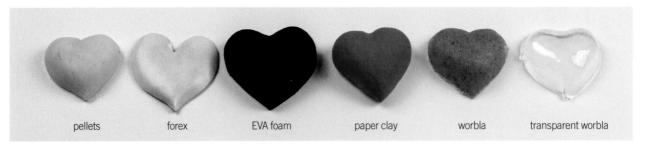

pellets   forex   EVA foam   paper clay   worbla   transparent worbla

Types of Thermoplastics

Here are a few of types of thermoplastics commonly used in cosplay. Paper clay, while not technically a plastic, can be molded similarly to EVA foam.

Thermoplastic Pellets

Boiling thermoplastic pellets in water makes them easy to sculpt. Once they are dry, you have a solid plastic shape.

Forex

Forex is a brand of white rigid PVC foam sheets used mostly for armor. You can shape it by heating it with a heat gun, but it is not recommended for small details. The heart example shown here is the maximum detail level for Forex.

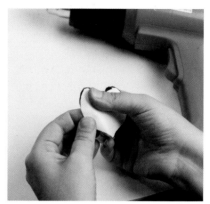

Worbla

Worbla is a popular brand of thermoplastic used for cosplay. It is a thin sheet of plastic that comes in a roll. It is nontoxic and available in lots of different colors. It can be used to trace shapes to form armor and props, and the leftover bits can be molded together by hand and reused for small details. Worbla is self-adhesive and can be easily applied by hand after warming it up with a heat gun. On the downside, it is a bit pricey and can have sharp edges if not handled properly.

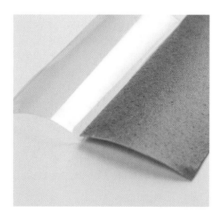

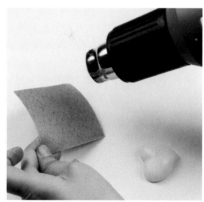

EVA Foam

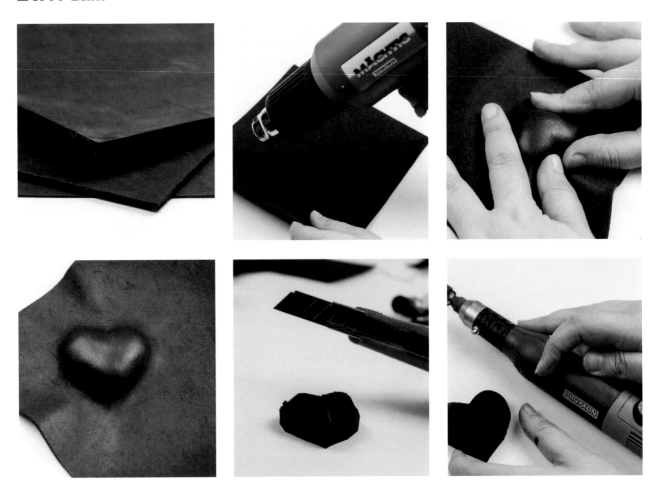

EVA foam comes in various colors and thicknesses and can be found in the form of garage flooring, yoga mats, and home insulation sheets. This foam is a lightweight and budget-friendly option for easy props and armors. It works best with contact cement. The most common thicknesses used in cosplay are 10mm, 5mm and 2mm. Thin EVA foam can be heated to transfer shapes and is cut easily with scissors. Thicker EVA foam can be shaped with a scalpel and then sanded into smooth shapes. You will usually get the smoothest finish by using a heat gun.

Paper Clay/Foam Clay

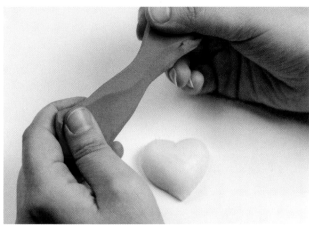

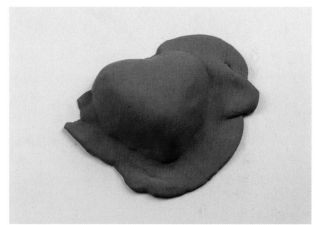

Similar to Play-Doh, paper clay is lightweight, flexible and easy to sculpt. It dries firm after just a few minutes, so it should be stored in air-tight plastic bags. You can get the clay in bulk and dye it yourself by mixing it with acrylic paints. Most types of paper clay do not work well with water. Shapes cannot be pushed together into a larger form; they must be glued.

Demonstration
Magic Ball

This illuminated magic ball is perfect for topping off a staff or weapon, or incorporating inside of armor.

MATERIALS LIST

clear plastic craft sphere, red acrylic paint and paintbrush, red transparent fabric, clip-on bicycle light (or any small battery-powered light)

1 Use a brush to roughly apply red acrylic paint inside the plastic ball shape. Let it dry.

2 Wrap a small battery-operated light in transparent fabric and turn it on. Here the fabric color is red, the same as the paint.

3 Stuff the fabric and light inside the ball and close it.

Now you can build this glowing orb as a prop inside a magical staff, affix it to a piece of armor or a big weapon, or pretend it's a magic crystal ball. The possibilities are endless!

Metallic Glove

Many armored characters need to have armored fingers as well. Here is a comfortable and long-lasting solution for armored fingers that can move freely and grip things with ease.

MATERIALS LIST

thin black fabric gloves, piece of card stock, scissors, thin EVA foam (black), white gel pen, silver acrylic paint, paintbrush, glue gun or other fabric adhesive

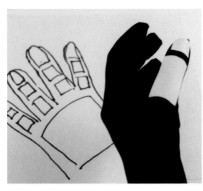

1 Trace your gloved hand on the card stock. Sketch out the shapes where you want the "metal" pieces to go, such as the knuckles and back of the hand.

2 Cut out the shapes and trace them onto black EVA foam using a white gel pen. Black foam is best for armor, but you can use any color foam you wish.

3 With a dry brush, make rough strokes of silver acrylic paint. Taper out the paint so that most of the color is layered in the middle of each piece.

4 While wearing the glove, glue the armor pieces onto your fingers and hand. If you are using a glue gun, it's best to use a mannequin or model hand to avoid burning yourself.

Your armored hand is ready for battle!

Metallic Fabric Coating

One of the most common ways to create cosplay armor is with paint. But cosplayers in Japan developed an alternative technique using a shiny metallic stretchy fabric. This is a long-lasting and effective way to make your costume look as if it is made out of metal.

MATERIALS LIST

EVA foam, stretchy metallic fabric, contact cement, scissors

1 Prepare your armor base out of EVA foam. Here I made two identical pieces of cosplay armor to coat with fabric. The base was constructed out of thick EVA foam. Decorative shapes cut from thin EVA foam were glued on top of the base with contact cement.

2 Select your fabric. Fabrics that will work for this technique include shiny vinyl fabrics, faux leather or cotton fabric that contains elastane. It is good for the fabric to be a bit stretchy so it falls inside all crevices. It is also important for the fabric not to soak in the glue.

3 I selected a shiny vinyl to cover the EVA base. Cut a piece of fabric that exceeds the size of your base. Apply a thin, even layer of contact cement over the entire surface of the EVA foam base, as well as the underside of the fabric. If you miss any part of the surface you may get air pockets, so make sure the glue coats both surfaces completely. Wait until the glue is dry to the touch before moving on to the next steps. (This could be a few minutes or longer, depending on the brand of contact cement you are using.)

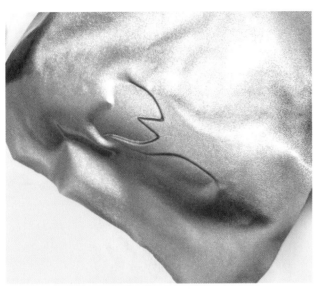

4 When the glue is dry (not tacky), carefully adhere the vinyl over the foam little by little. Work slowly to ensure that every part of the surface is covered. Press down so that the details show through.

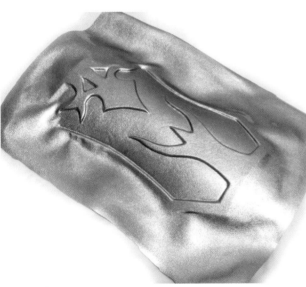

5 Continue adhering the vinyl to the EVA foam. It is important to avoid letting fabric wrinkles and air bubbles catch in the glue. Once you move past them, they become almost impossible to remove.

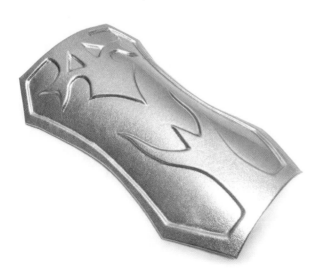

6 When the vinyl has been completely adhered, cut off the extra fabric with a pair of scissors. The end product is a long-lasting, smooth metallic finish that won't chip or crumble over time.

Fabric Armor in Action

This full-body suit of armor was created by contributor EDGE CAP
using the metallic fabric coating technique.

Rubber Spray on EVA Foam

You can also create an armored look using rubber spray and spray paint.

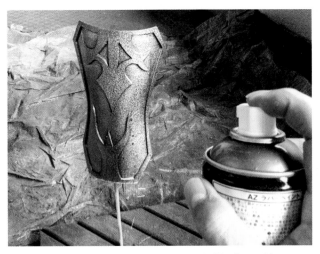

The piece of armor shown here was sprayed with silver rubber spray, also known as Plasti Dip. This spray-on rubber compound acts as a sealant on the EVA foam surface.

Now all it needs is some spray paint, and the painted-armor look will be complete.

Aging a Plastic Prop

You can turn any inexpensive plastic prop into a realistic-looking one using simple aging techniques. Simply cover the entire prop with black spray paint to erase any color, marks or blemishes. Then, using silver acrylic paint and a paintbrush, dry brush clean linear strokes along the prop's edges. Cover up any mistakes with black permanent marker, and voila—your lifelike prop is complete!

Be sure to thoroughly research your cosplay convention's or event's policies on realistic-looking weapons. Some conventions do not allow realistic-looking weapon props due to public safety concerns.

Simple Painting Technique

No matter what type of paint you are working with, your painting method should always be the same:

1 Priming

2 First Coat

3 Second Coat

4 Shading

5 Highlights

Don't Skip the Highlights

Unless your costume or costume detail is supposed to be a flat color, it is crucial to add highlights and shadows. Highlights are important to make your costume appear realistic and three-dimensional. If you don't add highlights, the costume can look flat, undefined and less realistic. Shading and highlights will help the surface of your props and costumes look more like they are professionally made and less like a simple piece of foam.

Painting Thermoplastics

It is possible to paint thermoplastics like EVA foam and Worbla, but they must first be primed. Make sure you read the instructions carefully before applying paint to make sure there will be no chemical reactions.

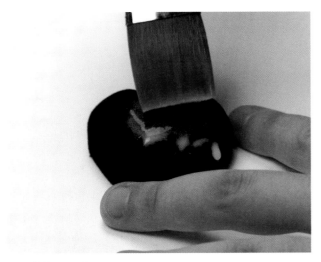

Applying Primer
This EVA foam heart is being primed with a mixture of wood glue and water in order for it to be able to accept paint. You can also prime most thermoplastics with rubber spray.

Primed EVA Foam
This is what freshly primed EVA foam looks like. It will need a couple of minutes to dry before it's ready for a coat of paint.

Primed Worbla
This is how a primed Worbla shape looks. It can be painted over after few minutes of drying time.

Tips on Painting Thermoplastics

Before use, make sure to shake the primers and paints well. Always spray paint in a well-ventilated area, and use a protective mask. Be patient and paint your works in thin layers. Leave enough time for each layer to dry well. Each base material does not necessarily need to be compatible with every primer or color. Test and compare all materials on a small area before proceeding to use them in crafting your cosplay.

Painting Fabric

Fabric paint, dimensional paint and acrylic spray paint are perfect for adding cool textures and shapes to light-colored cosplay fabrics such as cotton, linen, jute and silk. Most can be easily diluted with water and are washable once dry.

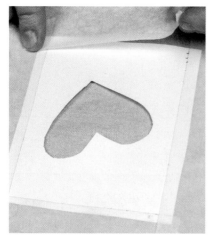

Secure the Stencil
Cut your stencils from thick paper or card-stock and secure them with fabric or masking tape, or any other mild adhesive tape.

Acrylic Spray Paint
Acrylic or regular spray paints work well on fabrics. Just make sure the paint is completely dry before you slowly peel back the stencil.

Brush on Fabric Paint
Using a paintbrush and diluted fabric paint, brush paint from the outside in for clean, crisp stencil shapes. Make sure the paint is dry before you lift the stencil.

Dimensional Fabric Paint
Three-dimensional fabric paint works wonderfully in cosplay costume design for imitating embroidery, jewelry, engravings or lace. It is best when used on top of see-through fabric or tule. Some common brands are Scribbles, Tulip and Marabu.

Coloring Fabric

One way of coloring fabric is to boil it in fabric dye. Make sure to read the instructions carefully, since different dyes have different procedures to follow.

You will need an old but usable pot. After dying your fabric, the pot should never be used for cooking again, but you can still use it for other crafting projects that require boiling water.

Pour Dye Into Boiling Water
To get better dye results, add extra dye. The amount of water and dye needed are stated on the packaging.

Add Cold Water
Pour cold water into the boiling water/dye mixture.

Dip the Fabric
Dip the fabric completely into the dye. You can use a wooden chopstick to keep the fabric submerged.

Simmer
Let it simmer for an hour. After an hour, with regular mixing, the fabric color will be more vibrant.

Before and After
Different fabrics can react in various ways to different dyes. This is why its always advised that you dye a sample first. After dying the fabric, it will need to be hand washed couple of times, then sealed with vinegar. Vinegar makes the colors more permanent and vibrant. IMPORTANT: This type of colored fabric should always be washed by hand!

Sewing Basics

Sewing can be done by hand (needle and thread), with a sewing machine or by connecting the fabric edges together with hot glue. However, if you want to create a long-lasting costume, learning how to use a sewing machine is your best option.

When sewing, always go slowly and carefully!

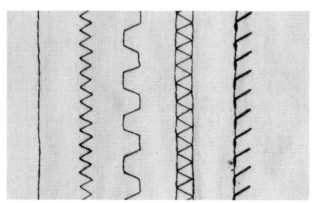

Types of Stitches

Most sewing machines offer a variety of sewing stitches for you to choose from. Some offer just the basics while others can offer over one hundred. The most common stitch is the basic straight stitch—this is what you will use most of the time for sewing costume pieces together. The zigzag stitch is great if you need a stronger connection. Then there are the many other types of decorative stitches for adding cool embellishments and embroidered touches to your costume.

Seam Ripper

Sewing is full of trial and error, so a seam ripper will be one of your best friends. If you make a mistake, just rip open the seams in question and redo the sewing until you are satisfied.

Sewing Inside Out

When sewing, you will always stitch the clothing inside out. Then, when the clothing is turned over, the seams will be clean and even. It's important to note that your clothes will look smaller and feel tighter when you flip them inside out and put them on. That is why you need to think ahead and always follow the saying: "Measure twice, cut once!"

One helpful thing to remember is that almost every fabric has a "face" and "back." The face is typically the prettier side of the fabric, while the back shows the rougher side. Always make sure you are looking at the back side while sewing.

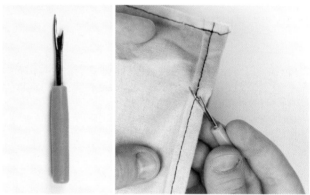

Hem

Every costume looks better with hems. A hem is a folded edge of fabric with a stitch in the middle.

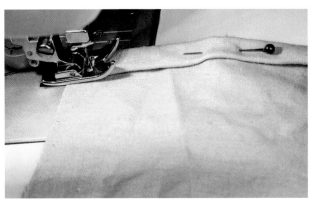

Pins

Pins are important because they hold everything neatly in place, but be careful to remove each pin before the machine reaches it.

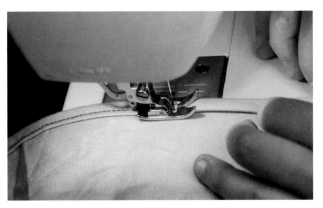

Consistent Lines

Strive for consistent straight lines while sewing. Keep in mind that this takes time and effort to perfect.

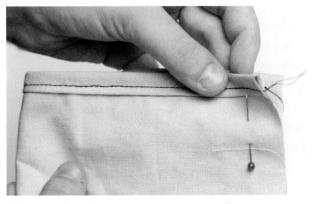

Closing the Sleeve

Once your hem is complete, you can begin closing the sleeve by working down the arm.

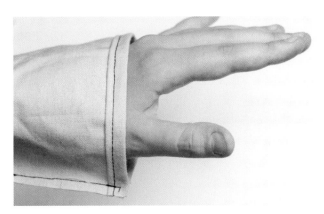

Finished Sleeve (Inside Out)

This is what a finished sleeve looks like while inside out, with the hem fold and the main stitch visible.

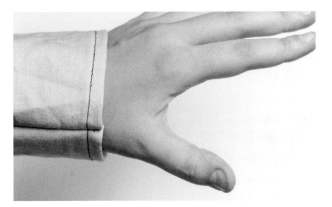

Finished Sleeve (Right-Side Out)

When the sleeve is turned right-side out, it is noticeably smaller. The hem folds are now invisible.

Sewing Curvy Shapes

Now let's step up the game and talk about curvy shapes. Skintight costumes rely on the ability to fit all the curves of the human body. These pieces are used to fit the female chest area, which is very important for many characters.

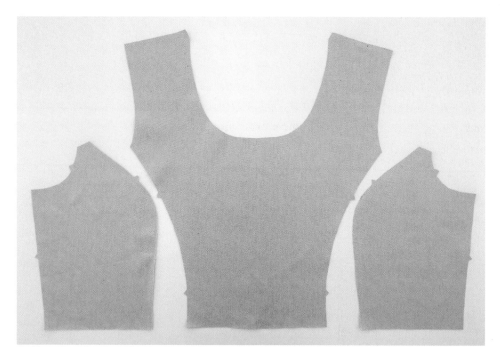

Female Chest Area
Skintight costumes rely on the ability to hug the curves of the human body. Here, these three pieces have been cut to fit the female chest area, which is common in many cosplay costumes.

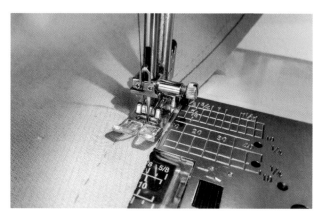

Stabilize Thin Fabric
If your fabric is thin and stretchy, such as spandex, sew a simple stitch (called a stay stitch) all the way around each piece. This will keep the fabric from stretching or distorting, making it easier to work with.

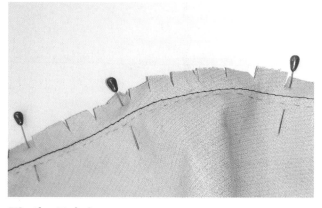

Pin the Fabric
Secure the parts you wish to connect with pins, just as you would when hemming a sleeve. Snip tiny V-shapes along the edges of both pieces to help the fabric fall neatly into a curvy shape.

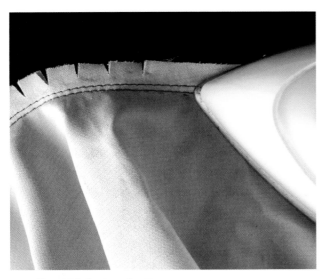

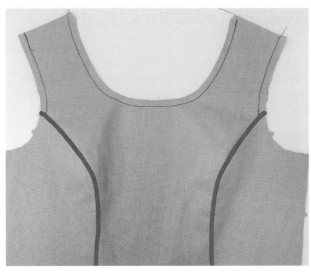

Dealing With Unruly Seems

If a curvy or a stubborn seam keeps falling out of place, use an iron on low heat to press the fabric down. This way the fabric will take in this curvy shape, and the costume will fit the body successfully. Just keep in mind that synthetic fabric can melt or burn if the iron is too hot.

Finished Female Chest Piece

The completed chest piece turned right-side out now allows for the cosplayer's natural curves to fit comfortably inside the seams. Male shirts can also have a variation of these seams for a closer fit.

Experiment With Sewing Stretchy Fabrics

In this example, the curved seams hug the body and also separate two different colors of fabric. It's important to note that it is much easier to sew skintight costumes if the fabric itself is stretchy. There are many types of fabric that are a blend of natural and stretchy fibers, such as elastane (or a Spandex blend), stretch denim, faux leather and many more. Try experimenting with combinations of fabrics to get the ideal look for your costume.

Ripped or Torn Edges

Finishing touches can sometimes make all the difference. With this easy trick, you can give your character that edgy, rugged appearance.

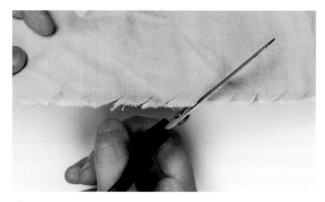

1 Start by diagonally cutting the edge of the fabric.

2 Cross-cut the fabric to make random shapes.

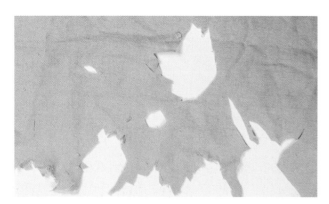

3 Add small and big holes for rugged results.

4 Use nail polish to keep the fabric in place. With some synthetic fabrics, you can even burn off the edges to seal them.

Now your character looks like they just stepped off the battlefield!

Cosplay Materials on a Budget

The costs of cosplay as a hobby can quickly add up. Luckily, there are lots of creative shortcuts you can take to create your favorite characters on a budget. Fabric can be pricey, but thrift stores offer unlimited possibilities to salvage and repurpose old clothes and gadgets into fabric and props for your cosplay. Turn old stockings into wig caps, or create vintage fabric by dunking white natural-fabric clothes in tea. Furniture refurbishment stores often have cheap fabric in bundles, such as textured fabrics and draperies, that you can make into gowns and dresses.

Let's turn this cheap curtain into a dress!

Salvage Plastic

To save on molding pricey thermoplastics, look for plastic containers in shapes that match parts of your character's armor, and use a glue gun to affix them. The gorget and shoulder pieces shown here were made out of plastic flower pots.

Repurpose Kitchen Tools

Besides fabric and plastic, you can get creative with common kitchen gadgets and tools like these ladles. Simply detach the bowls, and you've got a set of perfect epaulets!

Cat Ears

Making your own cat-like ears is great practice for creating custom ears that fit the color, shape and detail of your character—all on a budget.

MATERIALS LIST

plastic headband, two half-circle pieces of plush fabric for the inner ear (pink), two half-circle pieces of plush fabric for the outer ear (black), sewing machine, glue gun, ribbon, bells

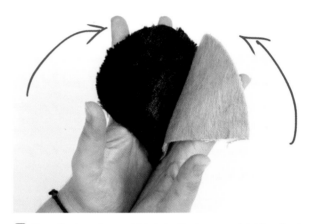

1 Gather your fabric—anything plush, fuzzy or furry will work great. The length of the base of each semicircle for the inner and outer ear pieces should be roughly 6½" (16cm). Remember that every fabric has a face (the fuzzy display side) and a back (the rough hidden side).

2 Place the two pieces of fabric for the inner ear (pink) and outer ear (black) face-to-face.

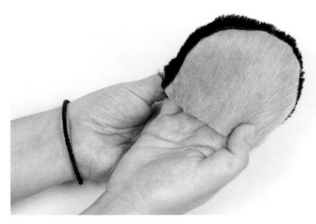

3 Set your sewing machine for a standard straight stitch setting. Sew around the fabric at least ¼" (1cm) away from the edge as shown with the dotted blue line.

4 Turn the ear inside out.

5 Fold the sewn semicircle in half with the black outer ear on the inside. You will sew the ear closed at the base and turn it inside out in step 7.

6 Sew along the base of the ear at least ¼" (1cm) away from the fabric edge. Do a backstitch (a second overlapping stitch) to further stabilize the seam.

7 Flip the fabric inside out again, and you have a fluffy cat ear!

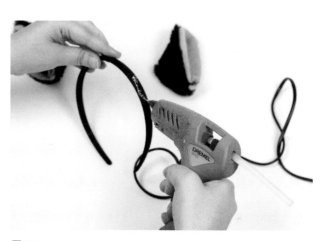

8 Use a glue gun to connect the headband to the ear. The glue is very hot, so be very careful not to touch it directly when securing the ear to the headband

9 Press firmly inside the ear to make sure it is securely and evenly connected.

10 Sew the second ear and secure it to the headband with a glue gun. You can leave the ears like this or add some bows and bells in the next step.

11 Tie a bow out of ribbon and glue it to the base of the ear. Finishing touches like bows and bells help to hide seams or loose threads inside the ear.

12 To add a finishing touch, glue a small cat bell to the base of the bows.

Your ears are complete! These jingly ears are the perfect addition to a cat-themed cosplay character. You can also customize this tutorial to make all sorts of animal ears.

Hair Clip Alternative

Bonus tip: Instead of a headband, you can try hot gluing the ears to hair clips. This way your ears will seamlessly fall into your hair or wig while staying perfectly secured to your head.

Cat Tail

Now let's make a matching tail for those fuzzy cat ears. Creating your own custom tail means that you can modify it to fit the height, color scheme and design of your character.

MATERIALS LIST

black plush fabric (approximately 20" × 6" [51cm × 15cm]), craft wire, fabric for filling/ stuffing, sewing machine

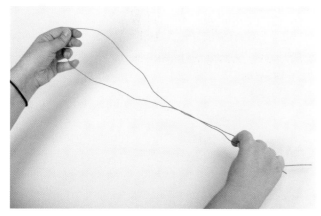

1 Cut a piece of 22mm gauge craft wire to size. The wire should be about twice as long as you want your tail to be. Here our wire is about 40" (102cm) so the finished tail will be 20" (51cm).

2 Twist the piece of craft wire into a long spiral tail shape.

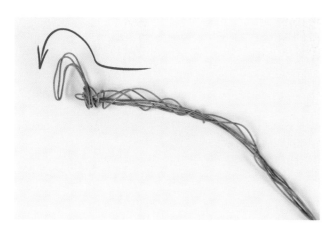

3 Add around 20" (51cm) more wire to wrap around the tail base and form a hook shape. You can attach this hook to a belt or to a piece of string around your waist. You could also just hook it between two layers of clothing to make it detachable (for example, between the pants and a belt.)

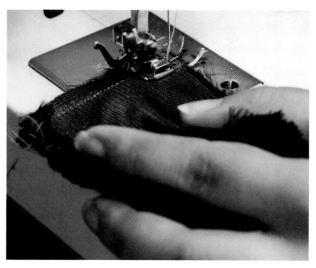

4 Cut a long piece of fabric about 20" (50cm) long. Here we are using the same fabric that was used for the outer ear fur in the cat ears demonstration. Fold the fabric in half lengthwise and sew one end of the tail closed. The other half of the tail should be left open.

5 Sew along the length of the tail. Use pins to keep the fabric folded in place as needed.

6 To turn the tail inside out, you need a pen or some scissors to push the outer fabric inside the tail shape. Push from the sewn end of the tail toward the open end.

7 Once the fabric is pushed all the way through, pinch the tip of the inverted fabric and pull it right-side out.

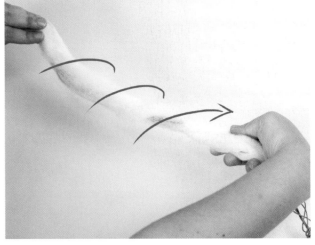

8 To make your tail more lifelike, it will need some pillow stuffing or other filling inside. Twist the stuffing around the wire, striving for even coverage.

9 Slowly feed the wire tail covered in stuffing through the opening you left while sewing.

10 To complete the look, add a bow or cat bell to match the embellishments of the cat ear demonstration.

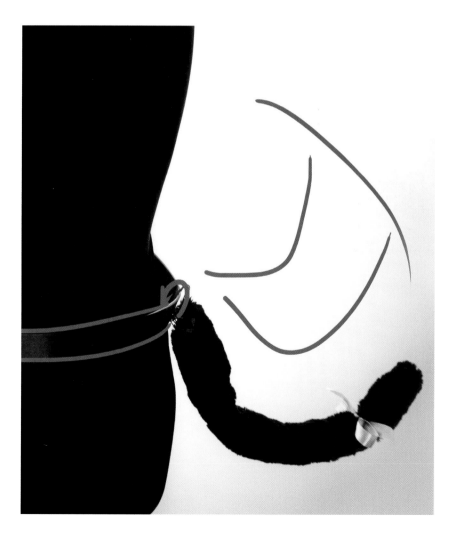

11 Fasten your tail onto a belt or simply tuck it under your costume shirt or flap. There are many ways you can affix a tail to integrate it into your costume. Also, because there is wiring inside the tail, you can pose it in any way you like—bend it up, down or even in a spiral.

On a final note, you can choose to close the upper seam of the tail if you wish. A simple hand stitch with some tail-colored thread or even a glue gun is all that is needed to close it up.

Demonstration
Claws

In this tutorial we will cover the process of making durable, custom-designed claws. You can wear these as a part of your glove for a seamless fingers-to-claws look.

MATERIALS LIST

wooden or plastic model hand, silicon glove, fabric glove, cardboard, scissors, glue gun and glue sticks, acrylic paints, paintbrush

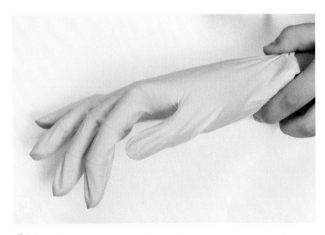

1 For this demonstration, it's important to use a model hand so that you do not burn yourself with hot glue. Cover the model hand with a silicone glove first to prevent the fabric glove from sticking to the model.

2 Cover the silicone glove with the fabric glove.

3 Cut a piece of cardboard in the shape of a long pointy claw—this claw is about 10" (25cm) long. Affix it to the index finger with lots of hot glue.

4 Use a hot glue gun to mold the shape of the claw, the base of the finger and details, such as veins, on top of the glove. These will be painted over in the following steps.

5 Choose three different acrylic paints for the claw, I have selected blue, gold and red. Paint the base half of the claw with an initial coat of blue. Acrylic paints bind nicely to dried hot glue.

6 Paint the top of the claw with gold and create a nice gradient where it overlaps the blue.

7 Paint the tip of the claw red for a dramatic look. Repeat the process on the rest of the fingers for a dramatic and creepy cosplay hand.

Demonstration
Simple Feather

Feathers are a must for winged characters. They also make beautiful costume adornments. The handmade feathers in this demonstration are not only easy and budget friendly, but cruelty-free.

MATERIALS LIST

craft foam, gel pen, scissors, glue gun, acrylic spray paint

1 Draw a rough leaf shape on 2mm craft foam with a gel pen. Make a few different sizes and shapes.

2 Cut out the shapes and snip various indents along the edges.

3 Continue cutting out details. Make sure not to cut too close to the center of the feather. This will make your feathers more likely to fold, snap in half or become damaged.

4 To create matching feathers, simply trace the desired feather onto another piece of craft foam.

5 With a glue gun, run a thin line of glue down the middle part of the feather to create a visible feather root.

6 Cover the feather with a base tone of acrylic spray paint. Here we used black.

7 Choose a second color of acrylic spray paint for the gradient—here we used gold. You can play around and add a third color or other unique markings with acrylic paint depending on your costume design.

Simple Horns

This technique will help you create horns of any shape and size. You'll begin by making a craft wire core, then use some paper tape for a lightweight frame you can easily paint over.

MATERIALS LIST

craft wire, plastic headband, paper tape, black spray paint, acrylic paints, paintbrush

1 Take your time and bend the craft wire into the shape of each horn. It may take some trial and error to get two matching horns in the size and shape you want.

    The craft wire will hold your horns in place and keep them from folding down or falling off altogether. Different horn shapes and sizes require different amounts of wire. Thin craft wire is ideal for making small sculptures such as cosplay horns. 22-gauge craft wire is optimal, but you can use similar wire gauges too. As a budget option, you can even use a thin wire coat hanger for the base of your horns—it is soft and pliable and can be easily shaped by hand. Avoid heavy duty wire, which may give you a headache after prolonged use due to its weight.

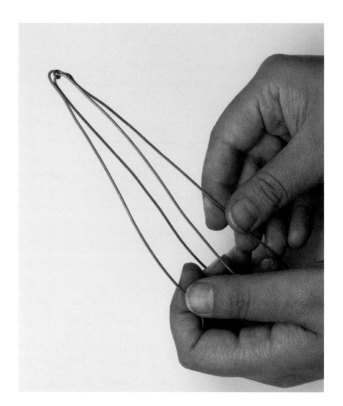

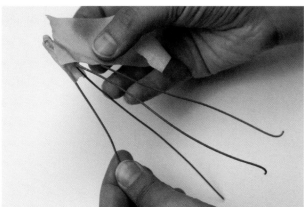

2 Slowly wrap the wire base of each horn with paper tape. You could also use duct tape, though it's a little stickier to work with.

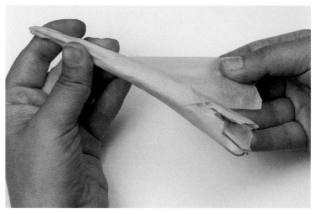

3 As you work, constantly check that both horns are symmetrical and similar in shape and size.

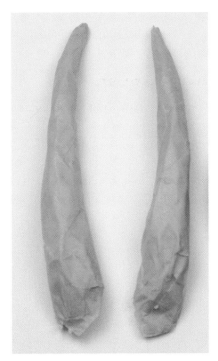

4 When you are finished, both horns should be roughly the same size and shape, but the inverse of each other.

5 Secure the horns to a plastic headband with more paper tape. Using the same tape you used to build the horns will give the piece a unified look. Headbands are great for this, because the horns can be easily removed from the headband later without compromising their shape.

6 As you work, try the headband on from time to time to make sure you have the placement accurate and even. When layering the tape, be careful to avoid any unsightly bumps or edges of tape that stick out of place.

7 Spray an even coat of black spray paint on the entire set of horns to prepare them for the painting process. Use black as a base color to help subsequent layers stand out, even if some of the colors get scraped off during wear.

8 Loosely apply brown acrylic paint at the base of the horns with a brush. Brush upward toward the tip of the horns.

9 Brush gold acrylic paint on the tips of the horns to add a bit of animal realism.

10 Try painting the headband in a color that is similar to your natural hair or wig. If you find that the horns slip on your head, use clips or clasps to help keep the headband in place.

11 Try combing your wig or hair in a way that conceals the plastic headband. Your can also glue hair extensions directly on the headband to create a full headpiece that you can put on or remove as a whole.

Cosplay Shoes

Custom shoes can be expensive or even impossible to find for your desired character. Fortunately, craft foam and EVA foam can be formed to cover your existing shoes and transform them into cosplay shoes. Here we'll make a futuristic looking shoe cover on top of an existing boot. Since there can be a lot of walking at conventions, it helps to start with a comfortable pair of shoes.

MATERIALS LIST

comfortable pair of shoes, duct tape, glue gun, permanent marker, thin craft foam, contact cement, elastic bands

1 Wrap the base of your boot in duct tape using the wrapping method shown in the previous demonstration. Based on your shoe cover design, draw the pattern lines with a permanent marker. Don't worry, the lines don't have to be perfect.

Barefoot Cosplay

If your character doesn't have shoes, self-adhesive padded feet stickers are a great way to protect the soles of your feet, yet still appear barefoot.

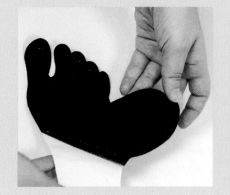
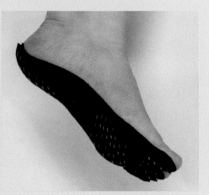

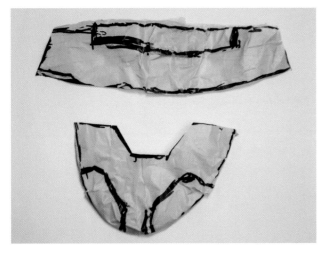

2 Use scissors to cut open the foot cover. We will use this pattern to transfer the shoe cover design to the foam for cutting. Be careful not to cut your actual boot!

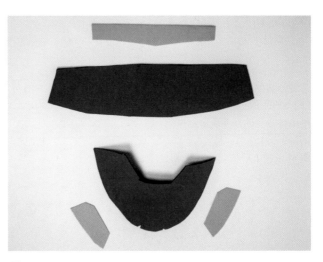

3 For this shoe cover, we are using 2mm craft foam, but for more lasting shoe covers, 5mm or 1cm thick EVA foam provides more durable, long-lasting cover.

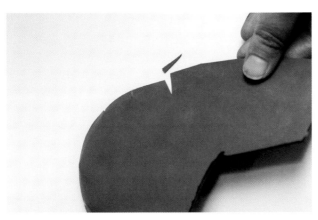

4 Cut the curvy top piece first. Make small V-shaped snips along the edge to help it bend around your boot in the desired shape.

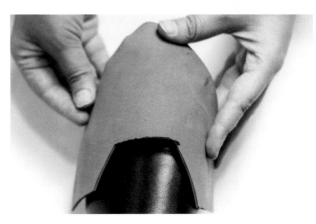

5 Gluing and shaping the shoe cover happens in several stages. Use a heat gun to make the foam more pliable. To get the shape of the cover right, trace the paper tape shapes onto the craft foam.

6 Trace all the shapes from the paper pattern onto several pieces of craft foam, including the decorative smaller pieces from the patterns. Use glue to affix the small decorative pieces in their designated places. If needed, you can strengthen the cover by gluing more pieces of foam inside the cover and onto the connecting parts of the base of the shoe cover.

7 When adding the decorative foam details, make sure you apply contact cement to the inside of the detail pieces (shown here in orange) before adhering them to the blue cover pieces. The glue must be completely dry to the touch before connecting the pieces.

8 Stabilize the lower edges of the foam with additional foam and contact cement. Gluing more craft foam bits will strengthen the inner bottom edge of the cover. This will help to protect the part of the cover that will be constantly sliding against the floor while you walk.

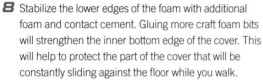

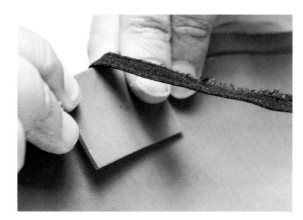

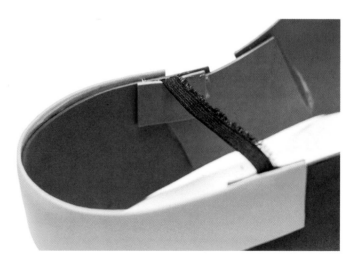

9 To keep the cover from falling off, attach two elastic bands to the inside bottom of the shoe—one under the heel, and one under the toes. Use contact cement to glue the bands between the edge of the cover and an additional small piece of foam.

Here is the completed simple shoe cover on top of the boot. In this exercise, we used foam colors that were the same as the finished shoe design,so we were able to skip the painting process. If you wish to further decorate the cover, refer to the section on painting thermoplastics for more information.

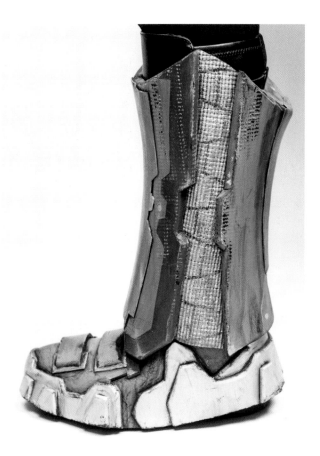

Detailed Painted Shoe Cover

Here is a more elaborate version of the shoe cover built with additional foam and painted to look like a boot. We used black EVA foam primed with black spray paint. The lower part of the boot was decorated with smaller bits of the same EVA foam with sanded edges. There is a piece of Velcro glued inside each shoe cover to make them easy to open.

Detailed Painted Shoe Cover With Shin Cover

Shin covers are made from 1cm EVA foam on the front and the back. A yoga mat was used on the sides because it's flexible and makes it easy to open and close the cover. There is a long Velcro strip hot glued to the inside of the yoga mat material and EVA foam so that they can close off the shin together. Texture and weathering effects were added to give the look of battle damage. Black EVA foam or black primer spray will keep this look authentic, even if the paint gets damaged at a convention or during transport.

Sewn Boot Covers

This is the most advanced and demanding tutorial. It requires a lot of patience and a little skill with a sewing machine. Keep in mind that you can try this technique with a glue gun, too, but faux leather usually does not work well with hot glue. It is important to find a thin faux leather, otherwise, your sewing machine might be weak to handle the thickness of the material. Of course, you may use other materials like cotton or synthetics, depending on the look of your character. The main thing to keep in mind is to re-check everything several times before you begin cutting your fabric.

MATERIALS LIST

comfortable boots, plastic wrap, duct tape, permanent marker, scissors, faux leather fabric, gel pen, sewing machine, jacket zipper, elastic bands, needle and thread

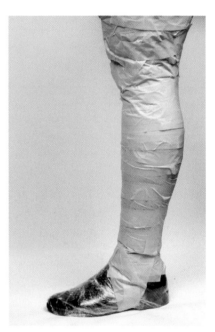

1 Select a comfortable boot that fits you well. Use this as the base model for your boot cover. Ideally, it should be similar in color to the color the covers will be.

2 Wrap the entire boot, including your foot and leg, in plastic wrap.

3 Wrap the boot in duct tape all the way to your shoe and under the foot like a stirrup.

Sewing Tips

- Sewing is tricky, so it is always advisable to buy some extra fabric. We tend to forget that every piece we cut off needs one additional centimeter in diameter. This extra fabric goes into each and every seam. If you cut the fabric exactly by your measurements without adding the extra diameter, you will create a piece of clothing that is one size too small for you.
- There are different types of needles for different fabric thicknesses, so make sure to use stronger needles for thicker fabric.

- Your sewing machine has a lower thread, and sometimes it can get tangled and mess up your work. To prevent this, make sure to always go on a slow and steady speed every time you are filling up a new batch of lower thread. This way the thread will be evenly placed and have less chance of tangling.

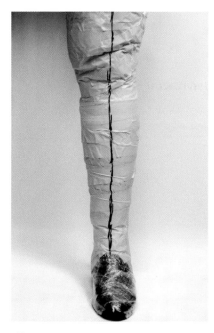

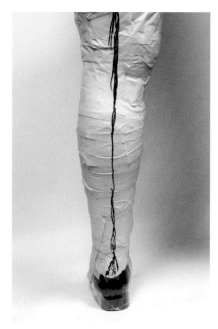

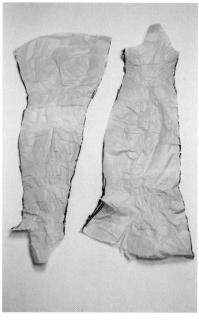

4 Draw a straight line up the front of the leg.

5 Draw a straight line up the back of the leg. It doesn't have to be perfect.

6 Cut along each line to form the pattern you will use for the boot cover.

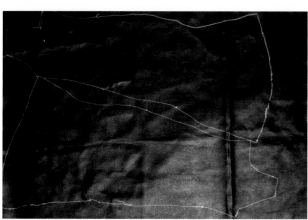

7 Place the duct tape pattern piece on top of the fabric of your choice. Here we are using a soft, stretchy faux leather in a dark brown color. Trace the patterns with a gel pen, adding at least 1cm on all sides. Make sure to press down tightly as you trace to get an accurate tracing.

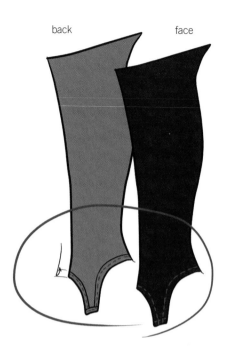

back   face

8 Fold the edges in around the fabric that you cut in step 7. (Remember, the gray fabric you see in this image is the back; the brown faux leather is the face.) Sew a seam along the entire edge of each boot cover.

9 Place the far edge of a long jacket zipper right-side down on the face of the fabric. First sew the far edge, then flip it over and backstitch the seam for a tighter connection. To make sure you are placing your zipper correctly and sewing it in the right way, a useful hack is to pretend the zipper is already sewn on by connecting the fabric and the zipper together with safety pins. This way you can place the zipper in the correct place, take a look at it from all angles, then slowly remove the safety pins, one by one, while following the trail of pins with the sewing machine.

10 Use pins to repeat the process on the other side of the zipper to connect the two pieces of fabric. Here we can see the trail of pins still visible on one side of the zipper, with the left part of the zipper being sewn into place. Keep the safety pins in place, and turn over the entire fabric zipper combo. It is easier to sew from the inside of the boot cover because the back of the faux leather is not smooth, and needles can pierce into it more easily. Always remember to pull out the safety pin and then sew down the edge of the zipper. If you don't remove the pins and your sewing machine needle hits it, the needle could break or there could be damage to your sewing machine. When you are done sewing the zipper edge from the back side, it should look something like picture no. 3. Keep in mind this type of sewing takes a lot of time and patience, and if you make a mistake, just use a seam ripper and try again.

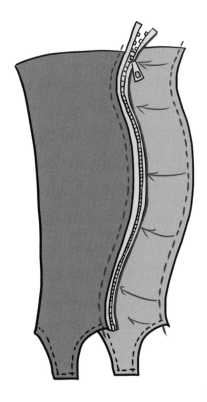

11 In this diagram, you can see that the zipper is supposed to be installed on the back of the boot cover. Make sure to always buy a jacket zipper, not an ordinary zipper. Jacket zippers can be opened at the bottom; regular zippers cannot. Also, make sure to buy a longer zipper, even if it is way longer than you think you need. Zippers are supposed to be cut to size after being sewn into place. However, before you cut the zipper to size, keep the zipper mechanism low, cut off the excess, and then hand stitch with needle and thread. It is crucial to hand stitch around the end of the zipper so that the zipper mechanism doesn't fall off by accident. Since the zipper is the most complicated part of the entire cover, we are attacking that first, and then proceeding to close the boot cover on the front.

12 Connect the front seam. The entire front of the boot cover is just one seam. Flip the cover inside out and sew along the front of the cover, starting at the bottom and working your way up to the top of the boot cover.

13 Sew elastic bands into the triangular bases of the stirrups to connect them underneath your boot while you are wearing them. When the boot cover is closed into a shin shape, you can sew a piece of elastic on the bottom of the cover. The boot cover should still be inside out as you sew each of the ends of the elastic to one flap on the bottom of the boot cover. The elastic will be going under the heel of the actual boot and will keep the boot and the cover held tightly together from below.

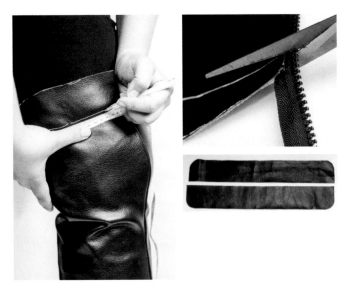

14 At this stage, this is what your boot cover should look like from the back, both unzipped and zipped. In the next step, we will add upper flaps that fold down for a nice dimensional look.

15 While wearing the boot cover, measure around the top of the cover with measuring tape to get the length of your mid-thigh. Cut out boot flaps from the extra faux leather fabric that measure this mid-thigh length plus 2cm. Cut the excess fabric and zipper off with scissors and hand sew the top so that the zipper doesn't fly off when you pull it up. The height of the flap can be the size of your choosing. Just make sure you cut curved edges on two of the four corners of each strip of fabric, as shown.

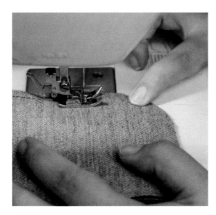  

16 Sew the two pieces face-to-face, then flip them inside out to the smooth faux leather side. Slowly sew along the outer edge of your new flap. Press the flap tightly and sew slowly along the curvy edge. This seam needs to be pretty as well as functional to keep your flap from being deformed. It is useful to sew all the way around so your flap looks like a solid piece that you can connect to the boot cover.

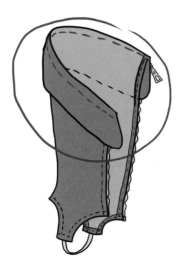

17 Connect the base to the thigh-high flap you completed in step 13. Place the flap to the cover and turn the straight side facing up. Connect the straight side of the flap by sewing it to the top of the cover, just like in the diagram. To prevent the flap from moving to the side while sewing, pin the middle of the flap to the front seem of the cover with a safety pin. This connects the final piece of the shoe cover in place, which you can later redesign to be bigger, smaller, decorated, made out of different materials, etc.

The final result is a cover that can go from svelte thigh-high boot to a pirate boot in one easy fold.

3 MAKEUP AND WIGS

Basic Skin Care

Our skin is a living, breathing part of our being. During cosplay, it can get dry, irritated, sweaty and prone to blemishes. It's important to keep your skin hydrated and clean between cosplays. There are may skin care products out there, such as lip balm, moisturizer, toner and pore-cleaning solutions. Experiment to find a combination that works for you.

Application Tools
Makeup sponges are used for applying creamy foundation. Makeup brushes can be used for both creamy products and setting powder.

Foundation
Foundations come in a variety of formulas (liquid and powder) and colors, so finding the best one for your skin type can take some time.

Setting Powder
If you use a setting powder or setting spray, your makeup can last the whole day.

Earth Tones
Earth tones can be used as eye shadow, but they also work well for creating shadows on the face.

Eyebrows
You can change the shape and color of your eyebrows with tools like eyebrow pencils, eyebrow brushes, tweezers, eyebrow filling wax and eyebrow powder.

Eye Shape
To change a shape of the eye, liquid eyeliner, mascara, pencil or false eyelashes can help.

Lips
Lipsticks can be liquid or regular. You can use lip pencils to draw out a new set of lips on your face that match your character.

Facial Massage

Facial massage is a perfect way to relax and keep your face youthful and glowing. Try these facial exercises with coconut oil or another facial moisturize. Focus on the parts of your face you deem to be most important.

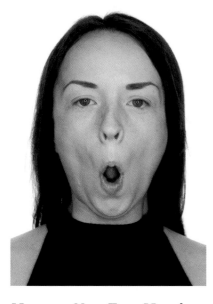 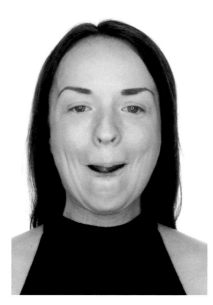 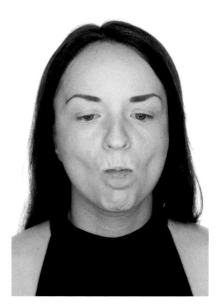

Massage Your Face Muscles

Like any other muscles, facial muscles will become toned and tighter with exercise. Daily face yoga can help sculpt your cheekbones and tighten your chin and jawline. All it takes is five minutes a day.

Contact Lenses

Contact lenses come with and without prescription, in many types and colors. They can be the perfect inexpensive detail to make your cosplay costume stand out. If you use them, make sure to keep them clean, keep them away from other chemicals and check the expiration date.

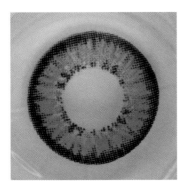  

Create the Illusion of Big Eyes
Lenses can be natural in diameter or larger to help create the illusion of bigger eyes, like a doll.

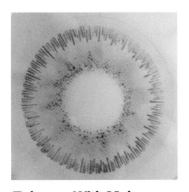 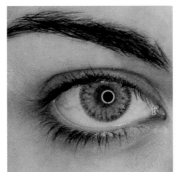 

Enhance With Makeup
Enhance the vibrant look of contact lenses with dramatic eye makeup.

Opaque Lenses
Opaque lenses provide an intense look. Combine them with strong makeup for an even more extreme vibe.

Makeup: Square, Masculine Face

Your face is a canvas, and by using makeup, you can transform yourself into pretty much anything you can think of—perfect for cosplay! In this lesson, we'll walk through some useful tips and tricks for creating a square, masculine face.

MATERIALS LIST

contact lenses (optional), glue stick, makeup sponges and brushes, primer, foundation, contour stick, concealer, eye pencil, black eyeliner, lip pencil, liquid lipstick

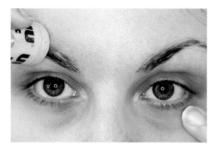

1 To begin, take a water-soluble glue stick and run it over your eyebrows in several layers to seal them in place. This makes them almost invisible when foundation or concealer is applied and will allow you to draw on totally new eyebrows during the makeup process.

If you plan on wearing contact lenses, make sure to sure to put them in before cleansing your face and applying any makeup.

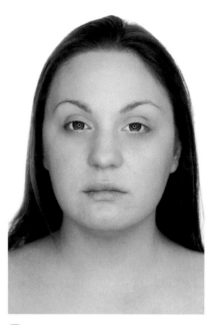

2 After moisturizing your skin, use makeup sponges to apply primer and foundation across your entire face including the lips, neck and upper chest.

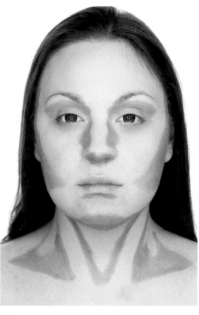

3 Use a contour stick to outline the areas that mimic a masculine look—make the area above the eyes more deep-seated, widen the chin base, square the jawline and create triangles that sharpen the cheekbones. Flex your neck and trace those lines for a more muscular illusion.

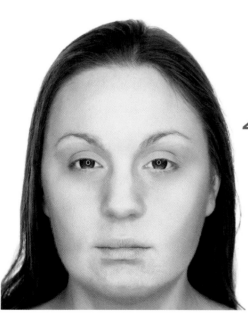

4 Blend the contour lines with a brush or blending sponge. You don't have to be super precise with the contour stick because the effects will be less visible after some blending. Repeat the contouring again, but with contouring powder or some skin-toned eyeshadow. Use various sizes of angled brushes for this.

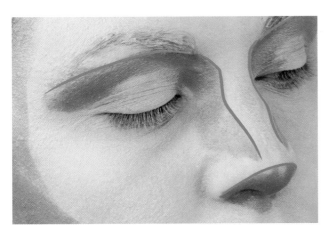

5 Draw lines on the outer nose and under the brow above the eye to make the nose look much thinner, and the eyes look more deeply set.

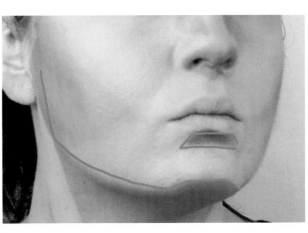

6 Use a darker-toned contour stick to create the illusion of a square jaw and a wide-set, square chin. Contour under the lower lip to create the illusion of a wider chin shape. Use shades darker than your own skin tone for both feminine and masculine face shapes. Draw harshly angled shapes for a masculine look and curvy shapes for a gentle, more feminine look.

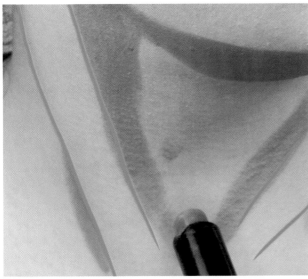

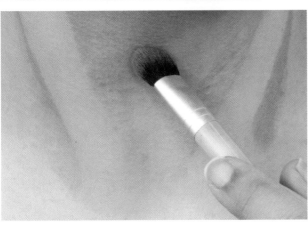

7 The trick to blending is to leave sharp lines visible at important points, such as your natural neck lines and the edge of your new jawline/chin.

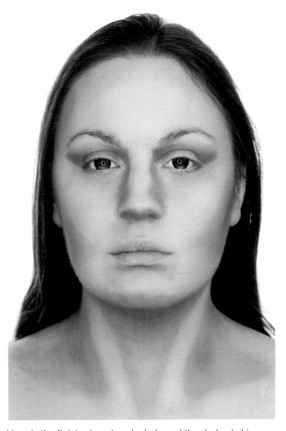

Here is the finished contour look. I used the darkest skin tone to achieve a dramatic and contrasted face with deep set eyes, jawline and neck lines. Keep in mind that this character has a less realistic, more cartoon-like face. For a realistic face, blend more and use several layers of setting powder to achieve a more muted look.

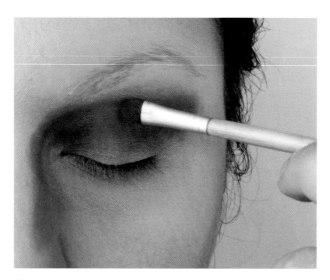

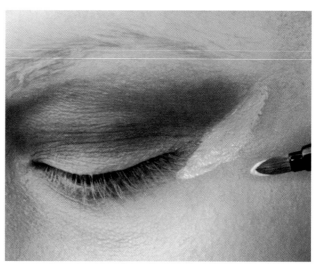

8 Add gradients and deepen the areas under the eyebrows to give the eyes a heavy shadow. Use a soft eyeshadow brush and the darkest shade in your contouring kit on the upper lid crevice edges. This enhances the illusion of a strong forehead.

9 If you make a mistake or need a clean line, use some concealer on a thin brush and blend everything except the desired line.

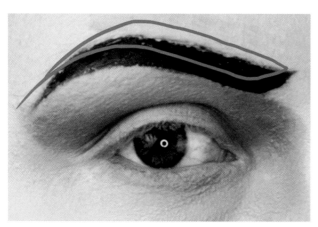

10 Once the natural eyebrow line is concealed, you can draw a new eyebrow on top with black eyeliner. (The green outline here shows the line of the original eyebrow.)

11 Use an eye pencil to construct your character's eye by drawing on a completely new eye shape while using your own eye shape as a base. Here I used eyeliner beginning just below the tear duct and pulled it along the eyelid and beyond in a cat's-eye shape. I used a white eye pencil on the waterline of the eye (the rim where your eyelid meets the eye) to help the eye appear smaller. No mascara was added on the lower lash line.

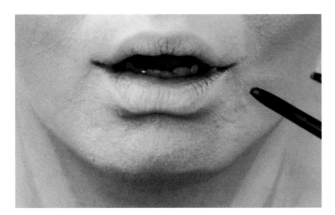

12 For masculine characters, use a lip pencil to draw a small line beyond the sides of the mouth. This creates the illusion of a wider mouth.

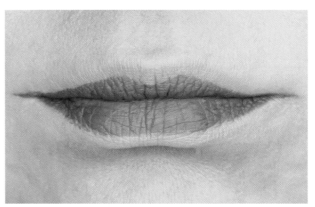

13 You can transform your lips into the shape of your character's by covering them in foundation and drawing them in as you like. Here I used red liquid lipstick to draw out thin, wide lips, and a brown lip pen to create a gradient from the corners of the lips. The real lip shape is concealed with foundation.

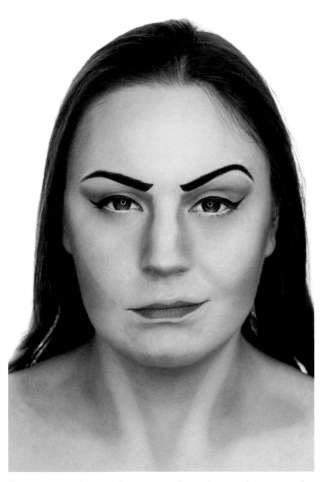

Every character has a unique personality and expressions to match. Practice them in the mirror to enhance the effects of your makeup.

Here is the finished character. Strong makeup like this looks great in photos, but make sure to take them in properly lit areas for the best results!

Makeup: Round, Feminine Face

In this lesson we will use makeup to paint a more round and slim face typical of feminine characters. Follow steps 1 and 2 from the previous demonstration before you get started. As always, remember to put in contact lenses before you cleanse your skin or apply any makeup.

MATERIALS LIST

contact lenses (optional), glue stick, makeup sponges and brushes, primer, foundation, contour stick, concealer, eye pencil, brow paint, black eyeliner, black mascara, lip pencil, liquid lipstick

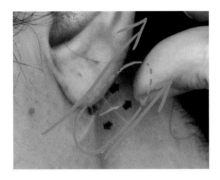

1 If you want a slimmer, tighter look to your face, you can try taping with cosmetic tape (sometimes called facelift tape) before applying makeup. First wash your face and neck. Then use the tape to tuck any loose skin behind the ear to create a slimmer profile to help the transformation.

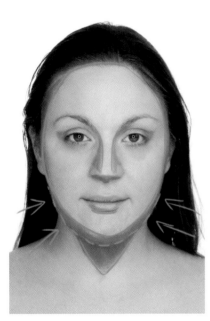

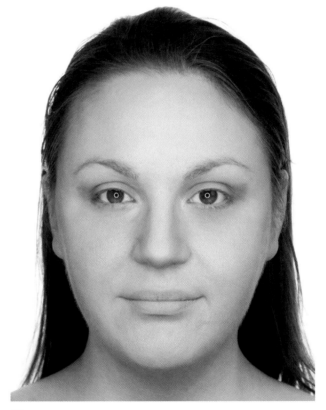

2 Using the same application techniques from the previous demonstration, form an elliptical shape around your face with a contour stick. You'll want to make an egg-shaped frame to create the illusion of a round face. Draw smooth, curved descending lines from the eyebrows to the nose. You are not going to draw neck lines for this character, but you will draw a fake shadow under your chin.

3 Blend the contour lines with a brush or blending sponge. You don't have to be too precise with the contour stick because the effects will be less visible after some blending. Repeat the contouring again, but with contouring powder or some skin-toned eyeshadow. Use various sizes of angled brushes for this.

4 Roughly draw out the shape of the eyebrow with an eye pencil. It is always helpful to use reference photos to match the look of your character.

5 An angled brush with some cream brow paint is all that is needed to fill in the shape. Some foundation and a thin brush will also help you make perfect eyebrow edges.

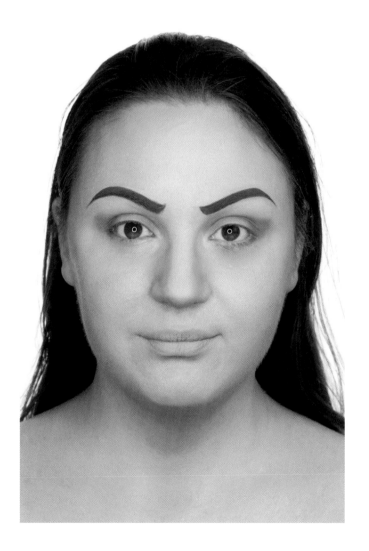

Here the eyebrows are complete. I drew them with brown color to match the soft color palette of this character. To get a softer face, try avoiding the darker shades of the contouring palette and, instead of darkening the face, use a highlighter powder to accentuate the feminine areas like the tip of the nose, the area below the eyes and across the middle of the face, and the forehead. Using highlighters will help you achieve a gentle glow on the face, which is more suitable for a feminine character.

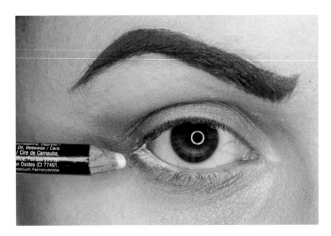

6 Once the eyebrows are complete, reshape the eye by extending it with a white eye pencil. The white will be the base for building the cat's-eye shape in the next step.

7 After extending the whites of the eyes, build the curvy cat's-eye shape on top with a lot of black eyeliner. Use black eye pencil inside the tear ducts, and black mascara on both the lower and upper eyelashes.

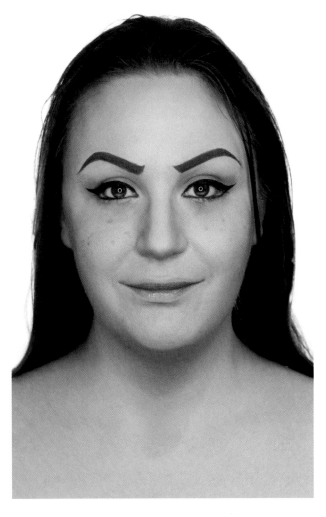

Here the eye shapes are complete. Depending on your own eye shape, you may try to build up on the shape by enlarging it with fake eyelashes, or drawing with the eyeliner away from the actual eye. For the feminine shape, it's always a good trick to draw upward-facing eyeliner tails. Since my eyes are naturally droopy, a thick line of eyeliner at the outer edges helps make the eye look more awake. Eyeliner takes some time and skill to perfect, but the results will be beneficial for drawing many different eye shapes.

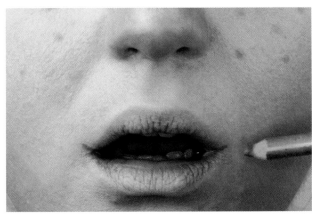

8 Use a brown lip pen to tap fake freckles across the cheeks, as well as to subtly widen the lines to the mouth.

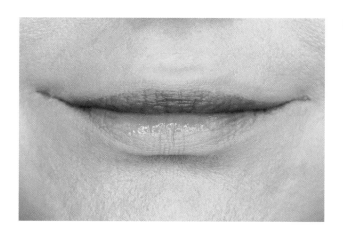

9 Apply liquid lipstick to shape the lips, then blend out the edges of the lips with some concealer. Apply a layer of lip balm for a youthful shine. Compared with the character in the previous demonstration, the lips are still smaller than the original shape, but the blurred edges and an oval lip shape enhance the feminine appearance.

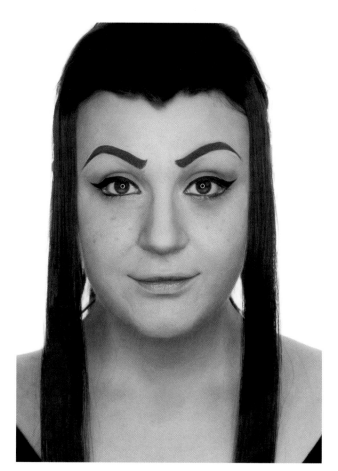

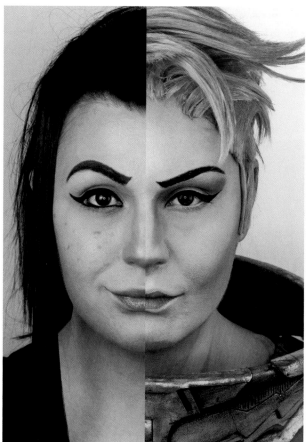

This character smiles by pulling both of her lip edges up at the same time while keeping her eyes wide open. Practice and memorize your character's expressions so you can replicate them at any time!

For the character of Brigitte from *Overwatch*, I had to keep my eyes open, my eyebrows lifted but relaxed, and both edges of my mouth pinched high to emulate her facial expressions and cheery, caring nature. She is the complete opposite of the confident and strong personality we showed in the previous demonstration, so her gestures and body language must complement her gentle looks.

Fake Tattoos

If your chosen character has a tattoo on their body, there are several ways you can create a temporary artificial replica.

Markers
For the cheapest solution, re-create the tattoo with any waterproof marker. These two tattoos were created with a generic CD marker and an office-grade fineliner.

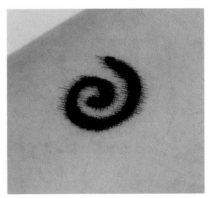

Test First
Always test the marker on your skin to see if it bleeds, how it will work for more detailed tattoos and if it can endure sweating.

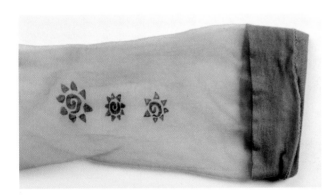

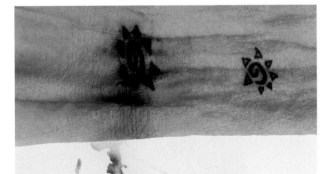

Try a Stocking Tattoo
If you don't wish to draw on your skin, try drawing the tattoo design on a stocking, and then cut it to wear as a sleeve. Stocking tattoos are reusable for several dress-up occasions. Be careful, though—if the tattoo sleeve gets wet with detergent or soap, the ink may bleed or smudge.

Printable Tattoos

For complicated designs, a great alternative is printable temporary tattoo paper. Just print your desired image and follow the instructions for applying it to your skin.

Tattoo Comparison

Here is a side-by-side example of temporary tattoos created with printable tattoo paper, waterproof markers and body paint.

Zombie Bite

Fake blood comes in many forms, has many uses and is perfect for taking your cosplay costume to the next level. Always test the product first to make sure it won't cause a skin reaction. You may also want to test if the product will actually wash out of your clothes or fabric.

MATERIALS LIST

special effects scar wax, liquid foundation, liquid blood, pipette

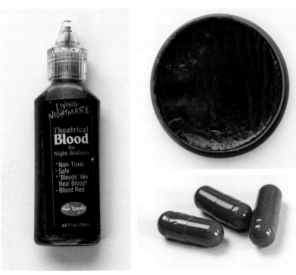

Fake blood comes in many forms—liquid (washable from skin and clothes), capsules (to fill your mouth) and paste. Decide which is best for the type of fake bruises and injuries you wish to create.

1 To create a fake zombie bite, use special effects scar wax blended with liquid foundation. You can find scar wax at any arts and crafts store. The brand I used here is Snazaroo FX Wax.

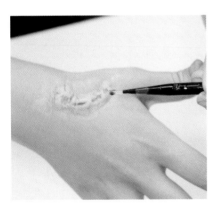

3 Use a pipette to drip some fake blood onto the fake bite.

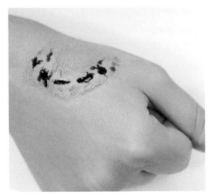

4 Fill in every indentation until each part looks like a little puddle.

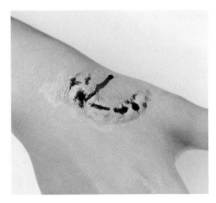

5 Tilt your hand to get a bleeding effect. If you are grossed out, it is a success!

Body Painting Basics

Many fictional characters have colorful skin and special body markings. To cosplay them, you might need to use body paint to get your desired effect. We will cover the basic techniques for applying color to your skin, as well as equipment, how to get the most out of your pigments and paints, and some alternative tips and tricks.

Types of Body Paint

Body paints come in many different types—oil-based, water-based, alcohol-based, powder pigment and liquid paints used in an airbrush. Alcohol-based body paints last the longest but are harder to remove. For casual cosplay, water-based is the way to go.

Body Painting Tools

Sponges are the most common tool for body paint application, but you can also use brushes or an airbrush system for a more professional approach. For casual cosplay, a regular makeup sponge will work well (even by professional standards) since it easy to use, easy to clean, and can be applied to any area of the face and body.

Sealing Body Paint

Sealing the body paint will prevent it from getting diluted with sweat, making it last longer at a meetup, a photo shoot or a convention. Professional makeup sealers are available, but a regular can of hairspray can do the trick just fine, and it's a budget-friendly option for large areas of coverage.

Moisturizing Is Key

Remember that makeup dehydrates skin and can also cause clogged pores. Always cleanse your skin and apply a total covering of moisturizer before you start layering body paint.

Body Paint Application

Applying body paint is a process that takes time and patience if you want perfect, long-lasting results. Application of body paint requires layering so you can get the most solid, visible color for your character's final look.

MATERIALS LIST

body paint, makeup sponge and brush, eyeshadow, hairspray or baby powder, baby wipes

MATERIALS LIST

body paint, makeup sponge and brush, eyeshadow, hairspray or baby powder, baby wipes

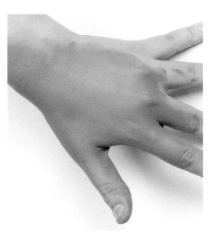

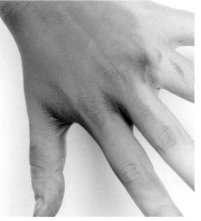

1 Apply the first layer of body paint with a makeup sponge. It will often look patchy and uneven at this stage.

2 Apply a second and third coat of paint to get a smooth, even look.

3 Apply dark gray eyeshadow to create some shading and expressive detail. Shade the areas between the fingers and accentuate the knuckle lines.

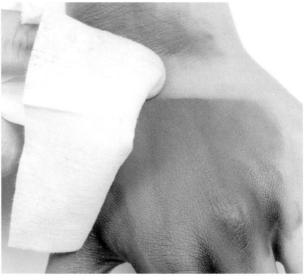

4 To seal the body paint and help it stick to the skin, spray it with an even coat of aerosol hairspray. This will also prevent the paint from transferring to your clothes. Baby powder is another alternative for sealing the paint.

5 You can use baby wipes for quick removal, but a thorough shower will remove all traces of the body paint. Remember to clean your makeup brushes and sponges after use, too.

Demonstration
Colored Nylon Glove

If you don't have the time to body paint, or you only have small areas that need coverage (such as your hands and feet), colored nylons are an easy alternative to body paint. Here we will hand sew a green nylon stocking into a glove.

MATERIALS LIST

colored nylon stockings, needle and thread, fake fingernails (optional)

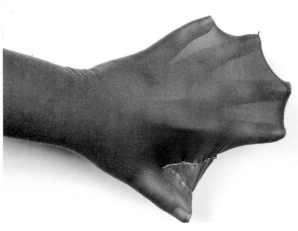

1 Place a colored stocking over your hand, and stretch your fingers to make sure there is enough fabric for a full glove. When hand stitching between your fingers, keep them wide apart at all time. This process can take a while because the stitching needs to be quite tight so the nylon doesn't tear apart.

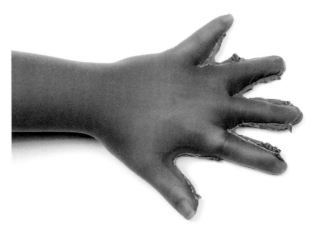

2 Stitch fully around each finger. If you run out of thread, make sure the previous stitching is well closed off with tiny knots, and then continue stitching with additional thread. After every finger is outlined with stitching, cut loosely once between the fingers with scissors, and trim any excess nylon hanging around the seams. Just don't cut too close to the seams

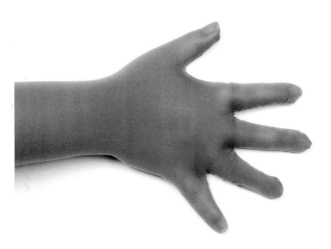

3 Turn the nylon glove inside out to hide the seams.

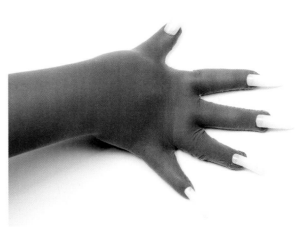

4 Glue some fake nails or claws to each gloved finger for a really cool effect.

Wig Tools and Hacks

You can use wigs, hair extensions, your own hair or a combination of all three to form all sorts of unique and expressive cosplay looks. Here we will start with the basics. Then we'll get into more detail in the wig-styling demonstration that follows.

Hair Clasps
Tiny claps are a must for hair and wig styling. You can buy or harvest these tiny hair clasps from hair extensions.

Wig Combs
Sew these tiny wig combs inside your wig to help it sit tight on your head.

Antistatic Comb
An antistatic comb is a crucial tool for combing your hair and wigs.

Thinning Scissors
Not all wigs come in a desired style, so a pair of hair thinning scissors (also called thinning shears) will be useful.

Hair Doughnuts
Hair doughnuts help shape your hair or fake ponytail into a bun. Use plenty of hairpins when working with wigs.

Hair Bumpers
Hair bumpers raise your hair or wig volume and help reshape your hairstyle.

Wefts

Wefts make up the building blocks of every wig, extension or fake ponytail. They come in all colors and sizes.

Sew a Wig from Wefts

You can create your own wig by sewing rows of wefts onto a blank wig base.

Fake Ponytail

You can purchase pre-made fake ponytails or wrap a weft sewn onto elastic mesh around a hair clip.

Hair Extensions

Hair extensions are also made from wefts, and you can insert them in the midsection of your hair to make it to appear longer.

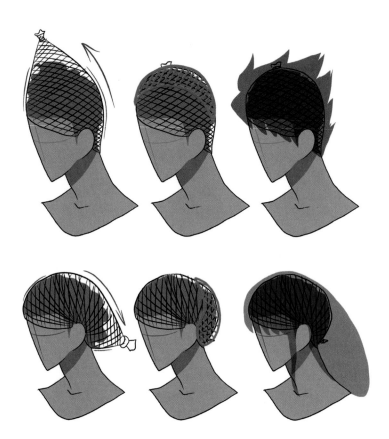

Dummy Head

If you want to style your own wigs, a dummy head is useful to have. This dummy is wearing a wig cap.

Put Your Hair in a Wig Cap

Before you put on a wig, it is best to put your real hair in a wig cap. Depending on the type of wig you have, you can do this in two ways. You can push your hair up inside the wig cap so it sits on top of your head, providing a nice base for a tall wig (top image). Or you can place your hair in the back, which leaves the head and forehead flat for a natural hairline (bottom image).

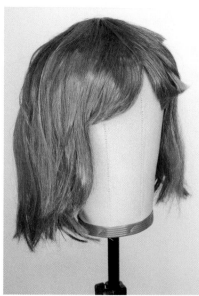

Reducing Wig Shine

If you buy a wig and it appears too shiny and reflective, you can reduce the unpleasant shine by coating it with baby powder, fabric softener, or both.

Dreadlocks

Pre-made dreadlock hair can be a useful tool for unique wigs. Tease them with a comb (image 2), use an old hair straightener on low heat to straighten them (image 3) or work them with hair wax for a firm shape (image 4).

Dye Your Wigs

You can also dye wigs to get the color you want. Alcohol-based markers are an easy solution (image 1). Or you can fill an airbrush with alcohol-based marker refills and spray the ink onto the wig (images 2, 3 and 4).

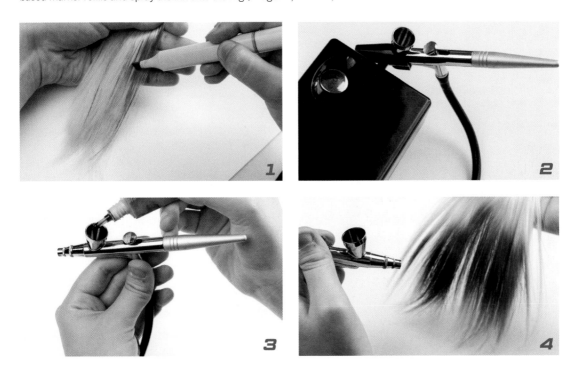

Demonstration
Styling a Wig

Wig styling can be an intimidating aspect of cosplay construction. It is quite different from other crafts, and it's often something that people have never done as beginning cosplayers. That being said, wig styling can be fun, it will improve your cosplay tremendously, and it is something that *anyone* can learn to do. If at first you don't succeed, just keep trying. You will learn from your past mistakes, and your wigs will get better with time and practice.

MATERIALS LIST

wig, sewing pins, dummy head, scissors, thinning shears, paddle brush, comb, freezing hairspray, bobby pins

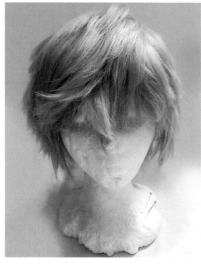

1 When selecting your wig, be sure that it is wefted in a way that will aid your intended hairstyle. I am styling a fluffy wig here, so it needs to be thick with a lot of volume on the top.

2 You will need a wig head or dummy to style the wig on, preferably one with a base, as this allows you to secure the wig while styling.

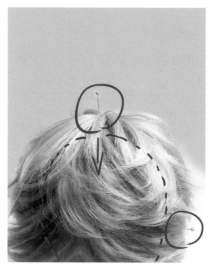

3 Use sewing pins to pin the wig into the dummy/wig head at the top and sides of the wig.

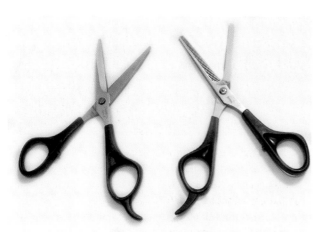

Scissors Make a Difference!

Thinning scissors (also called thinning shears) have an edge that allows hair to be cut at different lengths to help "feather" your wig and ensure that you do not get difficult, blunt edges. You will also need regular scissors for cuts that require a solid edge (mostly used during the cleanup phase).

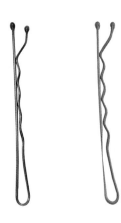

Brush and Comb

Different brushes have different uses. A paddle brush is gentle on wigs and useful for styling. Combs are ideal for smaller detailing on the wig.

Hair Spray

Hairspray and products used for wigs should not be "salon grade" or labeled as "gentle on real hair." Wigs do not absorb essential oils and other things that products concerned with hair health have in them. I prefer Got2Be Blued Freeze Spray.

Bobby Pins

Bobby pins are an important item to have on hand for wig styling. Bobby pins are bumpy on one side and closed at the end. They are helpful for holding hair in place for manipulating hair into positions while it is drying.

4 Spray the wig with hairspray and wait for it to dry before you start brushing. Brushing a hairspray-wet wig will make the wig stringy. The first step in wig styling is to find the shape of the wig. This means playing around with the hair and manipulating it with your fingers into the approximate silhouette of the hairstyle you are trying to replicate. In this example, we need more hair on the left side than the right side for the character's desired shape.

5 Use thinning scissors wherever possible to feather and layer the wig, thereby making it less choppy and easier to spike. Also, practice cutting at an angle with the blade tilted either toward or away from the scalp of the wig. In some cases you may want to cut straight across. If you do, always try to use thinning scissors for this. While trimming a wig, remember that you can always reduce length but you cannot easily add it back. When cutting, overestimate the length you need, and trim again if you need to remove more.

6 Once the wig is at its required length, styling can begin. A basic spike requires pulling the hair you want to spike between your fingers, then pinching at the tip of the spike. Spray lightly with hairspray, twist the tip of the spike lightly between your fingers and hold.

7 If the spike does not hold, try back-combing. While holding the spike between your fingers, comb the spike backward (toward the scalp).

8 This will create a "rat's nest," but don't panic. Simply brush the spike out, away from the scalp, and then try to spike it again. Repeat this process until the spike holds.

9 Use bobby pins to assist with holding spikes in difficult positions in place.

10 You can use sewing pins as well.

11 You can also use the palm of your hand to assist in creating shapes/masses that are more rounded (as opposed to triangular spikes). Use your palm to gently cup and support the section of hair you want to style. Spray the hair lightly with hairspray and hold until it dries.

12 Now that you have the foundational spikes/shapes of your wig, it's time to fine-tune and texturize! Texturizing adds depth and detail to a wig. Separate small sections or parts of spikes with your fingers. Spray a small amount of hairspray into your fingers and, while it is still wet, twist the tip of the section of hair between your fingers.

13 Bangs can make or break a wig because they impact how the wig fits your face. Try to avoid large and untextured bangs in the middle of the face. Adding a little bit of texture to bangs can help the overall look of the wig and your character makeup in general. Begin by separating out the bangs. Ideally you will want enough hair left for two distinct layers of bangs for texture.

14 Using the texturing method discussed in step 13, style the first and second layers of bangs.

15 Once all of the styling is done, take a step back from your wig. Examine it and spray with a misting of hairspray if you are satisfied. Allow it to dry and take a break. Come back to the wig later to clean it up. Cleanup means cleaning up your work section, but it also means gently cutting away stray strands of hair, specifically from the ends of the spikes.

16 When the wig is completely finished, spray once again with hairspray and let it dry. Your cosplay wig is now complete!

Cosplay Costume: A Quick Look

Now that you are familiar with basic cosplay terms, tools and materials, you can piece together a more complex costume. This lesson shows the step-by-step process for creating a fully constructed costume of Sylvanas Windrunner from *World of Warcraft*. The look took only few days to finish. It was made and worn by Tenshi Cosplay.

MATERIALS LIST

paper or cardstock for patterns, scissors, EVA foam, acrylic paints, paintbrush, colored thermoplastic sheet, heat gun, glue gun, Velcro, fabric gloves, elastic bands, cheap bra and leggings, fabric for cape

1 Sketch your costume design, and then draw it out in proper proportion on paper or cardstock. This will be your pattern. Cut it out with scissors.

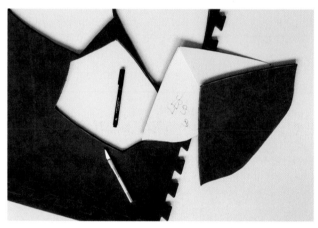

2 Use a black yoga mat to harvest EVA foam for the armored pieces.

3 Black foam is practical for this costume because you can paint directly on it. Plus, any potential damage that it incurs when you wear it will be difficult to see.

4 Paint the foam pieces with acrylic paint and a brush using a drybrush technique. Brush on clean lines for general markings, as well as light gradients for finer detail.

5 Melt a thin, colored thermoplastic sheet over the brightly colored foam with a heat gun to create the illusion of a rugged gemstone.

6 To easily get in and out of costume, Velcro can be a life saver. Most materials can be hot glued to Velcro, as was done here. Attach one side of the Velcro to the soft clothing, and the other side to the armored parts. This makes the armor detachable.

7 For the hand armor, glue EVA foam directly onto fabric gloves.

8 Cut feathers out of thin craft foam and then hot glue them to the armor as embellishments.

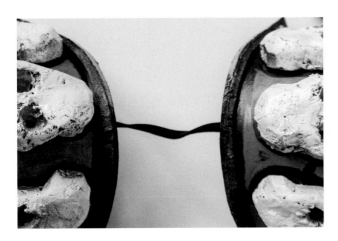

9 Hand carve Styrofoam skulls with a scalpel, then prime them lightly with some diluted wood glue. Paint on the details using basic acrylic paints. To create shoulder pads, heat EVA foam over a curved shape with a heat gun, then glue them to the skulls with contact cement.

10 Shape the breast plate by molding foam over a bowl. Use a heat gun to shape it.

11 Hot glue the breast plate armor to a cheap bra so that it securely fits against the body.

12 To further decorate the armor, shape thin, painted foam strips with a heat gun and apply them with hot glue.

13 Hot glue pieces of Velcro to a cheap pair of leggings—a few for each piece of individual leg armor.

14 Cut the bottom of a fabric cape into rugged, rough edges for an impressive final touch to the costume.

Here is the finished costume on display. Comfortable boots and a bow and arrow fashioned out of EVA foam complete the look. Try to identify the techniques applied to this costume that appear in this book.

Posing for Photographs

When you have spent a lot of time, effort and money on your cosplay costume, you should be able to wear it with pride and confidence. But having photos taken can be daunting for many of us. If you're camera shy, your instincts tell you to stand still and rigid, which results in disappointing photographs. Here are some tips to help you master different poses so that you can feel confident when having your photo snapped at your next event.

Poses to Avoid
In cosplay, standing still and looking straight ahead makes for a boring photo.

Master the Counterpose
To get a better pose for your photos, you just need two things: a counterpose and a mirror to practice. A counterpose is when your shoulders tilt one way, and your hips tilt the other.

Acute Counterpose
Here is a more extreme version of a counterpose. The hips are twisted more to the side, and the shoulders face forward.

Facial Counterpose
Combine your body counterpose with a counterpose of the face. Your eyes and eyebrows should face one direction, and your mouth the other.

Feminine Pose 1

This iconic and confident pose is reminiscent of the Sailor Senshi of *Sailor Moon*. It is a mix between strong and girly.

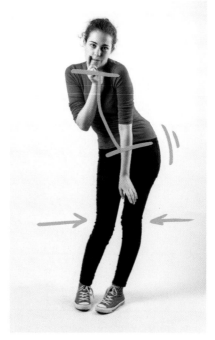

Feminine Pose 2

Curvy poses with connected knees and tilted hips are best for gentle, feminine characters.

Feminine Pose 3

By lowering the chin, the face looks more doll-like and the eyes appear bigger.

Warrior Pose 1

Fighting poses often contain a counterpose. Here one of the fists is positioned closer to the camera.

Warrior Pose 2

The superhero pose is one of the few poses that is straight-on and doesn't involve a counterpose. It is easy to do and creates a powerful, symmetrical image.

Warrior Pose 3

Research the weapons of your character so that when you pose holding them it will look historically accurate.

Practice Diverse Poses

By posing your body in diverse ways, you upgrade your whole look. Practice well-known character poses in the mirror to build confidence.

Point or Reach

By pointing or reaching for the camera, you create depth in the photo.

Get Flexible

Most of the best poses consist of unrealistic positions. Bend and flex around, and just keep experimenting.

Power Pose

This is another example of a symmetrical "power pose" used for characters of extreme strength and power.

Sitting Pose 1

Sitting poses follow to same rules as standing poses. Sitting in a normal manner does not make for an interesting photo.

Sitting Pose 2

By raising a knee, and shifting and bending the shoulders, you can make a sitting pose quite dynamic.

Composition: The Rule of Thirds

Properly composed photographs can give your cosplay pictures quite a professional look and feel. Plan out the angles and viewpoints of your shots using these cool tricks.

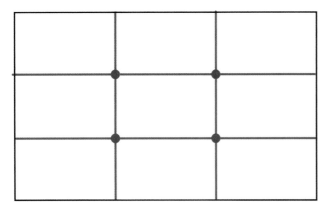

Turn On Your Camera's Grid
This grid divides the frame into thirds both horizontally and vertically. Almost all digital cameras and smartphones come with this grid for taking photos. Figure out how to enable it on your device and try it out.

Vertical Format
Here, the head, chest plate and belt are each contained by two intersecting points. Many photographers and graphic designers use this method to attract the viewer's eye to the important details of advertisements, billboards, flyers and other promotional materials.

Horizontal Format
The rule of thirds splits a rectangular area horizontally and vertically into nine sections. The four intersection points are considered suitable focal points because the eye is naturally drawn to these areas. Here the four points focus on the character's head, his chest, the staff and the light behind it. The fourth point is in shadow and is not a focal point.

Composition: The Golden Ratio

While the rule of thirds is a fine base for taking good photos, true artistic beauty lies in the composition of the golden ratio. The golden ratio is depicted by a single rectangle formed by a square and another rectangle. The pattern can be repeated infinitely. If you draw a curved line through the squares, you achieve a beautiful spiral shape similar to a nautilus shell that attracts the viewer's eye.

The Golden Ratio

The golden ratio is a mathematical principle behind many beautiful shapes in nature.

Seek Out Compositions in Nature

With practice you will be able to easily spot this composition in nature and other photos, and to plan it out in your own work.

Diagonal Composition

An easy and effective composition is when the whole image forms a diagonal line, corner to corner.

The Golden Triangle

The golden triangle is made up of four triangles that intersect at 90 degree angles. Your main compositional elements then fall within the triangles.

X-Shape Composition

When the subject forms an X, it is often a powerful character in a dominant pose.

Outdoor Photography

A good cosplay photo can make all the difference in showing off your costume and character. Outdoor photography can contribute to the mood of cosplay photos with natural lighting and the rich textures of buildings and nature. Follow these tips and tricks for a successful outdoor cosplay photo shoot.

Natural Lighting and Scenery

The outdoors can offer good, natural lighting and scenery and reduce the need for lots of photo editing. Cloudy weather offers the perfect outdoor lighting because there are minimal shadows.

before editing

Smartphone Cameras

If you have good outdoor lighting, such as a cloudy day, a smartphone can often take decent pictures if you don't have a DLSR camera.

after editing

Try a Reflector

If you lack light when you are shooting portraits outdoors, try adding fill light by redirecting sunlight onto your cosplayer with a reflector.

Studio Photography

Studio, or indoor photography, is used often in cosplay because it allows you to change backgrounds digitally and set up dramatic light effects and shadows.

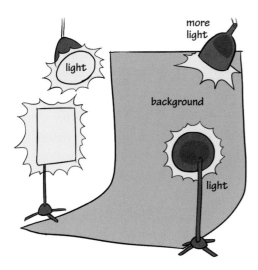

Basic Indoor Setup
Setting up a simple photo studio requires just a couple of things: a solid background (i.e. backdrop) and as many lights as you can find. Strong lighting will make all the difference in your photos.

Beginner's Budget Setup
This budget setup contains no lighting tripods, umbrellas or professional gear—just strong household lights and reflectors. The rig is held up by an iron ladder. The photography tripod is useful for stable shots. You can also take photos of yourself if you have a emote controller for your camera.

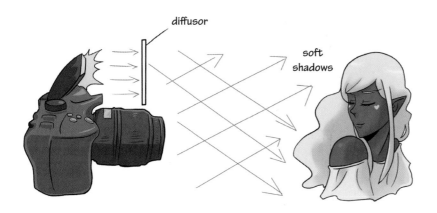

Soften the Flash
Avoid using a direct flash from your camera or smartphone. This can make your subject's skin look oily and cause harsh shadows. Cover the flash with a white piece of paper to diffuse the light and create nice, soft shadows.

Photo Editing Basics

You can use photo editing software such as Photoshop or other applications to enhance your photos. There are also lots of great free apps for your smartphone available that allow you to edit photos directly on your phone to correct simple imperfections and lighting.

Blur the Background
In this comparison, you can see the difference created by blurring the background and enhancing the light exposure.

Green Background
This cosplayer was photographed in front of green reflective fabric to help in the photo editing process. Since light tends to bounce off the background and transfer to the model, enhancing the green light gave us the green magic effect. (Cosplayer: David Landup; photo editing: Tenshi Cosplay.)

Gray Background
With a flat gray background, you can cut out the cosplayer and replace the background with anything you like. Here we added some dramatic backlight in the studio, and then used it to create the illusion of a window behind the cosplayer.

Color Theory

Understanding the basics of color theory is helpful for staging great photos. One concept that can help is complementary colors. Complementary colors are pairs of colors opposite each other on the color wheel: red and green, yellow and violet, and blue and orange. Use these easy tricks to improve your pictures.

Don't Overpower the Background

When working with complementary colors, their ratio is rarely equal. The relationship in color intensity is also not the same. In this red/green example, the red color on the costume is much stronger than the green colors in the background. The background should never overpower the character.

50:50 Color Balance

The blue/orange complementary colors are presented here in equal amounts. (Photo by Daniele Cosenza PhotoCosplay.)

80:20 Color Balance

This is another blue/orange example, but the orange covers around 80 percent of the surface, and the blue covers around 20 percent.

Convention Basics

Though tons of fun, conventions are often crowded events, and they can make you feel disoriented and confused if you get overtired or dehydrated. Keep a change of clothing in your bag so you can change out of your costume if you start feeling bad or overheated.

Carry a bag if your costume doesn't have pockets, and pack water!

Emergency Costume Toolkit
After many hours of walking, sometimes your costume or someone else's might start coming apart. These tools might may be helpful to bring along: a sewing kit, hot glue, scissors, super glue or a multitool. Check your local convention's website, as some items may be prohibited.

May I take your photo?

Yes!

Always Ask Permission!
Making friends at conventions is all part of the experience, but always ask for permission before taking someone's photo or getting physically close to them. Under no circumstances should you touch another cosplayer without their consent. If you are being touched without your consent, or if you feel harassed, inform security immediately and ask them to remove the person from the event.

Makeup Kit

At some point during an event, you will likely need to touch up your makeup or remove your contacts. These items should be in your bag at all times: a contour stick, fixing powder, contact solution and case, eyeliner, lipstick, eyelash glue (to fix your wig if it falls out of place or to stick details to the skin), a comb and bobby pins.

Personal Hygiene Kit

Personal hygiene is a crucial detail at conventions, especially when a space is crowded. Baby wipes, deodorant and a travel toothbrush can help you stay clean and fresh all day long.

First Aid Kit

Conventions can be unpredictable. It is wise to carry a small first aid kit (gauze, bandages and rubbing alcohol) in case you or someone you know is in need of aid.

Pet Cosplay

Cosplay can be a fun activity for the whole family, and sometimes even pets. If you choose to cosplay with a pet, the following rules are important.

ATTENTION!

If your pet is not comfortable outside or in big crowds, do not bring them to conventions!

I like to be at home, where it's quiet. Meow!

Make Sure Your Pet Can Move Normally

Costumes must not obstruct your pet's normal movement or breathing. This costume was made from soft plush fabric in the form of a simple cape with holes for front legs. Small Velcro tape keeps the cape closed in front.

When To Bring Your Pet

If your pet enjoys being outdoors and meeting people, a convention might be okay. Wait until you reach the venue to put your pet in costume. Make sure you bring water for your pet, and plan for a short stay.

Never adopt a pet solely for cosplay. Pets are not an accessory. They are meant to be loved and cherished for their whole lives.

Constant Checkups

Cuddles, water and treats should be a constant, as well as checking their mood and overall condition. Make sure your pet doesn't overheat. And if it gets to be too much for you or your pet, just leave.

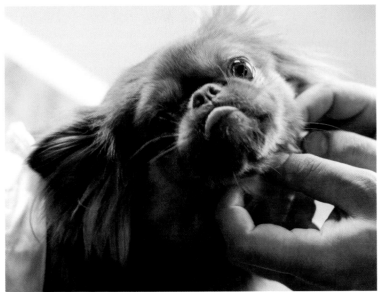

Show the Love

Your pet will need to know you appreciate them for doing cosplay. Shower them with love!

Use Light and Flexible Materials

Use an existing collar as a main fitting point for your pet's costume. Here we have a costume made from thin cotton strips, easy to open with Velcro. All pet costume fabrics need to be light and flexible, because animals constantly move around.

Adorn the Backside

Consider affixing costume details to your pet's back. Avoid sharp or heavy materials. This Leeloo Dallas costume from *The Fifth Element* is lightweight and simple. Perfect for a pet!

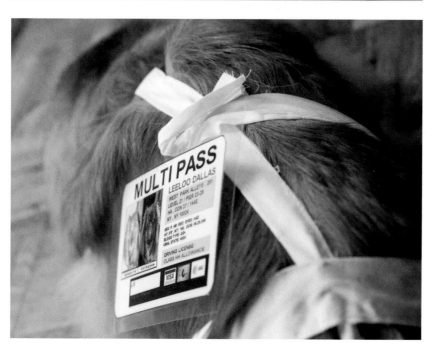

Tule

Stretchy light tule is a great, lightweight material to use as a base for a pet costume. Here, we loosely tied it around the chest and belly. Fake leaves were hand stitched to the tule to form a bush-like decoration. Now we have Poison Ivy from the DC Comics Universe!

Pet Photography

When taking pet cosplay photos, avoid bright flashes and any risky scenery. In this photo, we used lights that generated no heat.

Thanks, Leeloo!

A big thanks to our Pekingese puppy star, Leeloo, and her owner, Ivan, for these amazing photos! Follow Leeloo on Instagram @leeloo_the_cosplaydog.

Character: Poison Ivy
Cosplayer: Byalady Costumes
Photo by: Megin Zondervan
Facebook: byaladycosplay

Character: Alphonse Elric
Cosplayer: EDGE CAP
Twitter: ECAPT1

Character: Asajj Ventress
Cosplayer: Ferasha Cosplay
Sewing by: She&She
Prosthetics/props/editing by: Shunak
Photo by: Aleksandar Jovković-Guru
Facebook: ferashacosplay

Character: Sister of Battle
Cosplayer: JJ Cosplay
Crafting by: Bojan Kavedžic and
Marijana Miletić
Photo by: Vidak Kavedžić
(@the_cynical_photographer on Instagram)
www.flickr.com/vidakk

Cosplay crafter: Marijana Miletić
Photo by: Mina Petrović
Instagram: dreamstoneworkshop

Character: Marvin
Cosplayer: Laura Ducros
Photo by: Jerry LaRussa
Facebook: Rebel Among the Stars Studios

Character: 2B
Cosplayer: Tenshi Cosplay
Photo by: Julia Lazic
Instagram: tenshi_senpie

Character: Bakugou
Cosplayer: Twin Fools
Photo by: Neo Lynn Photography
Facebook: twinfoolscosplay

Character: Gwyndolin
Cosplayer: Yu xi
Sewing by: Katarina Nikolic
Crafting by: Marina Žikic
Photo editing by: Mina Petrović

Character: Zarya
Cosplayer: Mistiqarts Cosplay
Sewing by: She&She
Crafting by: Marijana Miletić
Wig by: Gesha Petrovich
Photo by: Daniele Cosenza Photography
Instagram: mistiqartscosplay

Index

Acknowledgments

These pages were brought to life by the extraordinary efforts of Tenshi, Marijana and Marina. I will never be able to express how grateful I am for their never-ending support and love. I also wish to say thank you to Teodora, Tesla, Sanja and Jovana Sretenović for being my rock and for always lending a hand in trying times.

Dedication

I dedicate these pages to the people behind the costumes who always work hard—you have my love and appreciation. To the design team at She&She creative studio, Marina Andelković and Ana Barajević, who helped raise our small cosplay community to the heights of perfection. To all the contributors who gave their time and effort to create this guidebook with me. And most of all, to the ever-growing global cosplay community. Spread love and positivity, care for each other, and remember to live through imagination, because that's truly what cosplay is all about.

About the Author

Mina "Mistiqarts" Petrović is an award-winning cosplayer, fashion designer, author, manga artist, instructor and body-positivity activist from Belgrade, Serbia. Mina is well known in the cosplay world globally, and she recently served as an official cosplay judge for Belgrade Chibicon in 2018. In 2009, she was awarded first place for cosplay alongside Bojan Vukadinović at the Japanizam cosplay convention. She has since been an active member of the Sakurabana cultural organization and has helped organize many events and conventions in Serbia over the last decade. She is the author of two books, *Manga Crash Course* (2015) and *Manga Crash Course: Fantasy* (2017), and she continues to attend world-wide conventions as an international cosplay judge, panelist and lecturer.

YouTube — Mistiqarts
DeviantArt — Mistiqarts
Twitter — Mistiqarts
Instagram — mistiqartscosplay
Facebook — MistiqartsCosplay

IMPACT Books
An imprint of Penguin Random House LLC
penguinrandomhouse.com

Copyright © 2019 by Mina Petrović

Printed in the United States of America

10 9 8 7 6 5 4 3

ISBN 978-1-4403-5479-3

Edited by Sarah Laichas
Designed by Clare Finney
Production managed by Debbie Thomas

Ideas. Instructions. Inspiration.

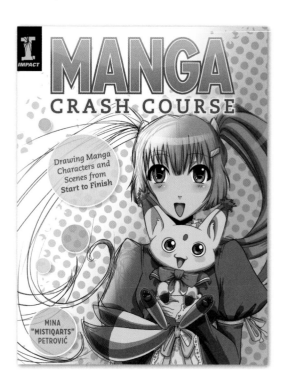

IMPACT